AF432596

The Verses of Legend Hanuman Ji

Mrigendra Bharti

Published by Sellbrochure Entertainment Vymish, 2024.

While every precaution has been taken in the preparation of this book, the publisher assumes no responsibility for errors or omissions, or for damages resulting from the use of the information contained herein.

THE VERSES OF LEGEND HANUMAN JI

First edition. June 4, 2024.

Copyright © 2024 Mrigendra Bharti.

ISBN: 979-8227174130

Written by Mrigendra Bharti.

Table of Contents

Dedication

the Divine Presence of Hanuman Ji,

In reverence and gratitude, we dedicate this book to you, Hanuman Ji, the embodiment of boundless love, courage, and wisdom. Your divine presence shines as a guiding light, illuminating the path of our spiritual journey and offering solace in times of uncertainty.

Your unwavering devotion to Lord Rama serves as an eternal reminder of the power of love and loyalty. With each leap across the ocean and every act of selfless service, you inspire us to deepen our connection to the divine and to serve others with humility and compassion.

In the face of adversity, your boundless courage and strength inspire us to overcome our fears and challenges, reminding us that true greatness lies within the depths of our hearts. Your humility and integrity serve as beacons of light, guiding us to walk the path of righteousness with grace and dignity.

As we journey through the pages of this book, may your divine presence infuse our hearts with love, courage, and wisdom. May your teachings inspire us to embrace the virtues of devotion, courage, humility, integrity, compassion, and forgiveness, leading us towards a life of purpose, joy, and divine grace.

With deepest reverence and devotion,
Mrigendra Bharti
Jai Hanuman! Jai Shri Ram!

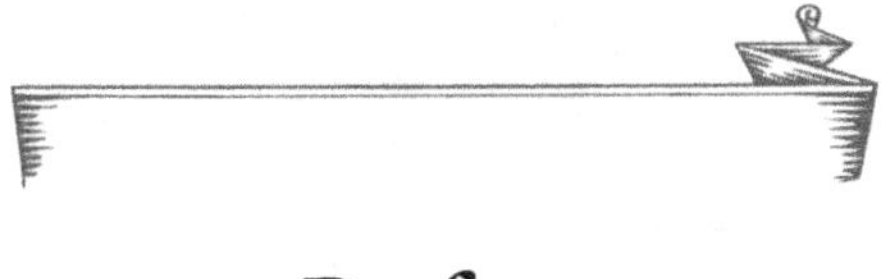

Preface

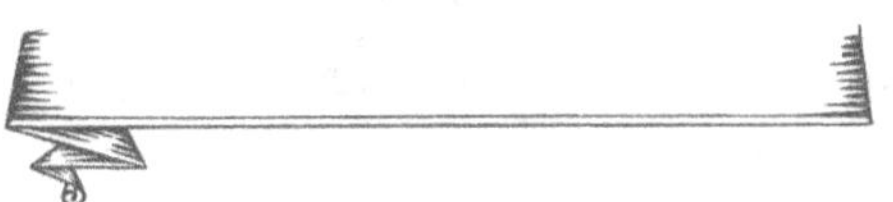

In the vast tapestry of Hindu mythology, few figures stand as tall and as revered as Hanuman ji. From the epic pages of the Ramayana to the sacred chants of devotees, his presence looms large, embodying the virtues of devotion, courage, and selflessness.

"The Verses of Legend: Hanuman Ji" is not merely a recounting of mythological tales; it is an immersive journey into the heart of one of Hinduism's most beloved deities. Within these pages, readers will discover a treasure trove of stories, teachings, and insights that illuminate the timeless wisdom of Hanuman ji's character.

This book seeks to explore the multifaceted persona of Hanuman ji, from his miraculous birth to his heroic deeds in service to Lord Rama. Through meticulously curated verses, anecdotes, and reflections, readers will come to understand the depth and breadth of Hanuman ji's influence on Hindu mythology and spiritual consciousness.

Each chapter of "The Verses of Legend: Hanuman Ji" delves into a different aspect of Hanuman ji's character and significance. From his unwavering loyalty to Lord Rama to his boundless compassion for all beings, Hanuman ji emerges as a beacon of light in the darkness of ignorance and despair.

As you embark on this odyssey through the annals of mythology, may you find yourself enraptured by the timeless wisdom and grace that Hanuman ji embodies. May his teachings inspire you to cultivate the virtues of courage, humility, and devotion in your own life, and may his eternal presence serve as a guiding light on your journey of self-discovery and spiritual enlightenment.

Jai Shri Ram!

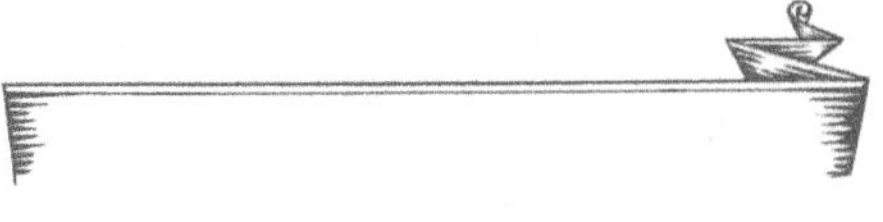

Foreword

In the timeless expanse of Hindu mythology, amidst the grandeur of celestial battles and divine interventions, few figures command the reverence and adoration that Hanuman ji does. His saga is not merely a story but a living legacy—a testament to the enduring power of faith, devotion, and selflessness.

In "The Verses of Legend: Hanuman Ji," we embark on a sacred pilgrimage through the hallowed halls of myth and legend, guided by the radiant presence of Hanuman ji himself. Within these pages, we are beckoned to explore the depths of his divine persona, to unravel the mysteries of his birth, and to witness the splendor of his heroic deeds.

Hanuman ji's tale is a symphony of valor and virtue, resonating across the ages with the clarion call of righteousness. From his humble origins as the son of Vayu, the wind god, to his monumental feats in the service of Lord Rama, every aspect of Hanuman ji's existence is steeped in significance and symbolism.

As we immerse ourselves in the verses of Hanuman ji's legend, we are confronted with the profound truths that lie at the heart of his story. Through his unwavering devotion to Lord Rama, Hanuman ji teaches us the transformative power of love and surrender. Through his boundless courage and strength, he inspires us to overcome even the most daunting of obstacles with faith and fortitude.

But perhaps most importantly, Hanuman ji embodies the timeless values of loyalty, humility, and service—a shining example for all who seek to walk the path of righteousness. His selfless dedication to the cause of dharma serves as a beacon of hope in a world often shrouded in darkness.

As we journey through the verses of Hanuman ji's legend, may we be reminded of the eternal truths that his story imparts. May we draw strength from his indomitable spirit and find solace in his unwavering presence. And may we, like Hanuman ji, strive to live lives of courage, compassion, and devotion.

It is with deep reverence and gratitude that I invite you, dear reader, to embark on this sacred odyssey through the realms of myth and legend. May the blessings of Hanuman ji illuminate your path and guide you ever closer to the divine.

Jai Shri Ram!

Prologue

In the vast expanse of time, where myth and reality intertwine, there exists a realm where gods and demons clash, where heroes rise and fall, and where the forces of light and darkness wage an eternal struggle for supremacy. It is within this timeless tapestry of myth and legend that the story of Hanuman ji unfolds—a story that transcends the boundaries of time and space to touch the hearts of believers and seekers alike.

The tale of Hanuman ji begins in the celestial realms, where the gods dwell in splendor and the heavens resound with the echoes of divine hymns. Born to Anjana, the celestial nymph, and Vayu, the wind god, Hanuman ji emerges into the world with a destiny written in the stars—a destiny that will lead him on a path of glory and greatness.

From his earliest days, Hanuman ji displays signs of his extraordinary powers, performing feats of strength and valor that astound even the mightiest of beings. But it is not until he encounters Lord Rama, the embodiment of dharma and righteousness, that Hanuman ji's true purpose is revealed.

Drawn to Rama by an unbreakable bond of love and devotion, Hanuman ji pledges his allegiance to the prince of Ayodhya, vowing to serve him with unwavering loyalty and dedication. Thus begins a journey that will take Hanuman ji to the farthest reaches of the earth and beyond—a journey filled with trials and tribulations, victories and defeats, but always guided by the light of dharma.

In the pages that follow, we will witness the epic saga of Hanuman ji unfold before our eyes, as he embarks on a quest to rescue Sita, the beloved wife of Lord Rama, from the clutches of the demon king Ravana. Along the way, we will encounter gods and demons, sages and warriors, each playing their part in the cosmic drama that unfolds.

But beyond the battles and the triumphs, the miracles and the wonders, lies a deeper truth—a truth that resonates with the very essence of existence itself. For in the story of Hanuman ji, we find not just a mythological tale, but a timeless parable—a parable of devotion, courage, and selfless service—a parable that speaks to the highest aspirations of the human soul.

As we journey through the verses of Hanuman ji's legend, may we be inspired by the example of his life, and may we strive to embody the virtues that he so magnificently exemplifies. For in the heart of every devotee beats the spirit of Hanuman ji—a spirit that knows no fear, no doubt, and no defeat.

Jai Shri Ram!

Acknowledgment

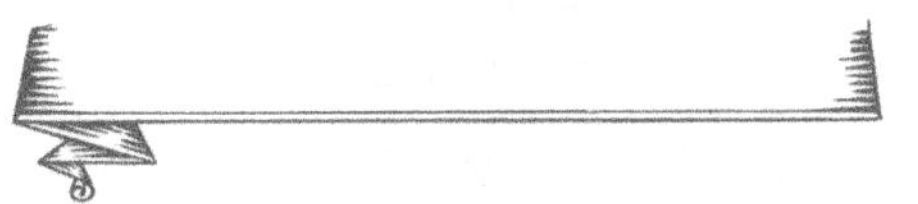

As I sit down to pen these words, I am overwhelmed with a profound sense of gratitude to all those who have supported and inspired me on this journey of writing "The Verses of Legend: Hanuman Ji."

First and foremost, I offer my deepest thanks to Hanuman ji himself, whose divine presence has guided me every step of the way. Your boundless love and grace have been my constant companions, illuminating my path and filling my heart with inspiration.

I am eternally grateful to the sages, saints, and storytellers of ancient India, whose timeless wisdom and sacred scriptures have provided the foundation upon which this book stands. Your teachings continue to resonate through the ages, reminding us of the eternal truths that lie at the heart of existence.

To my family and friends, whose unwavering support and encouragement have sustained me through the highs and lows of the writing process, I offer my heartfelt thanks. Your belief in me has been a source of strength and motivation, and I am forever indebted to you for your love and kindness.

I am also deeply thankful to my editors, advisors, and colleagues, whose expertise and insights have helped shape this book into its final form. Your invaluable feedback and suggestions have enriched the content and enhanced the clarity of its message.

Last but not least, I extend my heartfelt gratitude to the readers, whose curiosity and passion for mythology have inspired me to embark on this literary journey. It is my sincere hope that "The Verses of Legend: Hanuman Ji" will serve as a source of inspiration and enlightenment for all who seek to explore the depths of Hindu mythology.

In offering these acknowledgments, I humbly recognize that this book is the result of the collective efforts and contributions of many individuals. To each and every one of you, I extend my deepest appreciation and thanks.

Jai Shri Ram!

Introduction

In the hallowed annals of Hindu mythology, amidst the celestial abodes of gods and goddesses, there exists a figure whose name resounds with reverence and adoration—a figure whose presence is felt in every corner of the cosmos. That figure is Hanuman ji—the epitome of devotion, courage, and selflessness, whose legend transcends time and space to touch the hearts of millions.

In "The Verses of Legend: Hanuman Ji," we embark on a sacred journey into the heart of Hanuman ji's divine saga—a journey filled with tales of heroism, wisdom, and boundless love. From his miraculous birth to his awe-inspiring exploits in the Ramayana, Hanuman ji's story is a tapestry woven with threads of divine grace and mortal endeavor.

But who is Hanuman ji, and why does his legend endure through the ages? To understand the significance of Hanuman ji, we must delve deep into the sacred scriptures of Hinduism, where his name is uttered in hymns of praise and his deeds are celebrated in epic verse.

Born to Anjana and Vayu, the wind god, Hanuman ji emerges into the world with a destiny written in the stars. Endowed with extraordinary powers from birth, he embarks on a series of adventures that will take him to the farthest reaches of the earth and beyond. But it is his encounter with Lord Rama, the embodiment of dharma, that sets Hanuman ji on the path to greatness.

Drawn to Rama by an unbreakable bond of love and devotion, Hanuman ji pledges his allegiance to the prince of Ayodhya, vowing to serve him with unwavering loyalty and dedication. Thus begins a journey that will test the limits of his strength and the depths of his faith—a journey that will ultimately lead him to the pinnacle of divine glory.

In the pages that follow, we will explore the many facets of Hanuman ji's character and significance, from his miraculous feats of strength to his profound wisdom and compassion. We will witness the epic battles he wages against the forces of darkness, and the sacrifices he makes in the name of righteousness.

But beyond the myths and the legends lies a deeper truth—a truth that speaks to the very essence of our existence. For in the story of Hanuman ji, we find not just a mythological tale, but a timeless parable—a parable of devotion, courage, and selfless service—a parable that resonates with the highest aspirations of the human soul.

As we embark on this sacred odyssey through the realms of myth and legend, may we be inspired by the example of Hanuman ji's life, and may we strive to embody the virtues that he so magnificently exemplifies. For in the heart of every devotee beats the spirit of Hanuman ji—a spirit that knows no fear, no doubt, and no defeat.

Jai Shri Ram!

Author Biography

Mrigendra Bharti, born on June 29, 2004, in South Delhi, India, is a multifaceted individual recognized as the owner of Mrigendra Bharti Group InfoTech India Co. Pvt Ltd. Beyond his entrepreneurial endeavors, he is a distinguished music producer, director, and a budding writer.

EMBARKING ON HIS PROFESSIONAL journey at a young age, Mrigendra Bharti's visionary leadership has led to the establishment of several successful ventures, including Croma Music Series Entertainment, Sellbrochure, Fauget Innovative, and more.

WHAT SETS MRIGENDRA apart is his early initiation into the world of business. His foray into the unknown realms of entrepreneurship began during his 10th-grade years, where he delved into the music industry. This initial venture laid the foundation for subsequent achievements, showcasing his dedication and resilience.

HAVING HONED HIS SKILLS in music, Mrigendra Bharti not only demonstrated significant growth in his craft but also expanded his professional network. His passion extends beyond music, encompassing app and website development, as well as graphic design.

FUELED BY HIS CREATIVE aspirations, Mrigendra established the Mrigendra Bharti Group, a company specializing in website and app development. Currently, he collaborates with a dedicated team, collectively working on ambitious projects that promise innovation and excellence.

MRIGENDRA'S JOURNEY serves as an inspiration, particularly for today's students, highlighting the potential of youthful determination and the ability to transform innovative ideas into successful businesses. As he continues to make strides in various domains, Mrigendra Bharti remains a dynamic force, contributing vibrancy to the realms of business, music, and technology.

Hanuman Ji's Birth and Childhood

The Enigma of Birth

In the celestial realm, where the heavens meet the earth and the gods reign supreme, a divine drama unfolds—a drama of love, sacrifice, and destiny. At the heart of this drama lies the enigmatic figure of Hanuman ji, whose birth is shrouded in mystery and wonder.

As the son of Anjana, the celestial nymph, and Vayu, the wind god, Hanuman ji emerges into the world with a destiny written in the stars—a destiny that will shape the course of history and transcend the boundaries of time.

But even as the gods rejoice at the arrival of this blessed child, whispers of prophecy fill the air, hinting at the challenges and trials that lie ahead. For Hanuman ji is no ordinary being—he is destined for greatness, destined to play a pivotal role in the cosmic drama that is about to unfold.

As Hanuman ji grows from infancy to childhood, his divine heritage becomes increasingly apparent, as he performs feats of strength and valor that astound even the mightiest of beings. But amidst the wonders and marvels of his upbringing, there is a sense of longing—a longing to discover the true purpose of his existence, to unravel the mysteries of his past and embrace the destiny that awaits him.

But amidst the trials and tribulations of his journey, Hanuman ji remains steadfast in his quest, guided by the wisdom of his divine heritage and the teachings of his beloved mother Anjana. With her words echoing in his ears and her love burning in his heart, Hanuman ji presses on, his faith unshakable and his spirit unyielding.

And so, as the days turn into weeks and the weeks into months, Hanuman ji's quest for self-discovery becomes a journey of transformation—a journey that will not only reveal the truth of his origins, but also forge him into the greatest hero the world has ever known.

For in the heart of every hero lies the fire of righteous purpose, the flame of divine guidance, and the strength of unwavering determination. And as Hanuman ji continues on his quest, he knows that with each step he takes, he draws closer to the destiny that awaits him, closer to the truth of his existence, and closer to the realization of his true potential.

Little does he know that the challenges he will face, and the sacrifices he will be called upon to make, will test the limits of his courage and the depths of his faith, and ultimately, lead him to embrace his true destiny as the greatest hero of all time. But for now, as he stands on the threshold of greatness, Hanuman ji knows only one thing—that his quest has only just begun, and that the adventure that awaits him will be the greatest of his life.

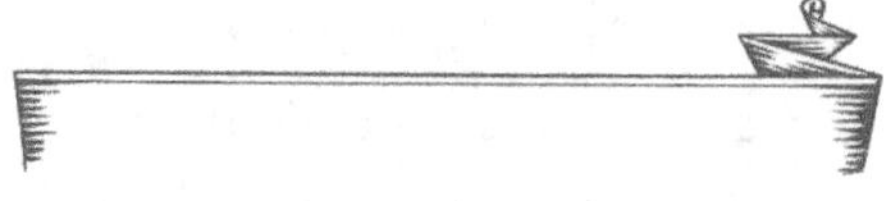

Into the Abyss

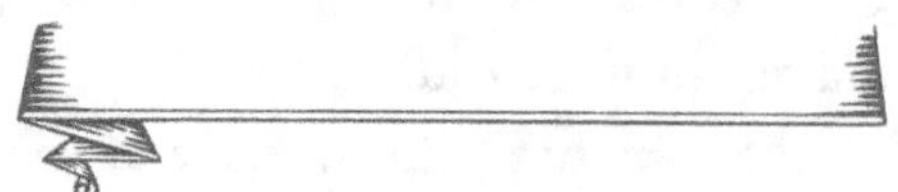

As Hanuman ji delves deeper into his quest for self-discovery, he finds himself drawn into the depths of the abyss—a realm of darkness and despair, where the shadows whisper secrets of forgotten truths and the echoes of ancient battles reverberate through the void.

Undeterred by the daunting landscape that surrounds him, Hanuman ji presses on, his determination unyielding and his spirit unshakeable. For he knows that within the darkness lies the key to unlocking the mysteries of his past, the secrets of his origins, and the truth of his destiny.

As he navigates the treacherous terrain of the abyss, Hanuman ji encounters beings both ancient and powerful—entities whose very presence sends shivers down his spine and whose words carry the weight of centuries. From the guardians of the underworld to the spirits of the forgotten realms, each encounter tests Hanuman ji's resolve and challenges his understanding of the world.

But amidst the darkness, there are also glimmers of light—beacons of hope that illuminate the path ahead and guide Hanuman ji on his journey. From the wise counsel of celestial sages to the gentle guidance of benevolent spirits,

Hanuman ji finds solace in the knowledge that he is not alone, that his quest is supported by forces greater than himself.

And so, with each passing day and each new challenge overcome, Hanuman ji grows stronger, wiser, and more determined than ever to unravel the mysteries that lie at the heart of his existence. For he knows that only by confronting the darkness within himself can he hope to emerge into the light, to fulfill his destiny, and to embrace the heroism that lies dormant within his soul.

But as he delves deeper into the abyss, Hanuman ji becomes increasingly aware of the dangers that lurk in the shadows—dangers that threaten to consume him, body and soul. For the abyss is a place of temptation and temptation, where the desires of the heart can lead one astray and the whispers of the mind can lead one into darkness.

But Hanuman ji is no ordinary being, and he knows that his destiny lies not in the embrace of darkness, but in the triumph of light. And so, with each step he takes and each challenge he faces, he draws closer to the truth of his existence, closer to the realization of his true potential, and closer to the destiny that awaits him.

For in the heart of every hero lies the fire of righteous purpose, the flame of divine guidance, and the strength of unwavering determination. And as Hanuman ji continues on his quest, he knows that with each step he takes, he draws closer to the destiny that awaits him, closer to the truth of his existence, and closer to the realization of his true potential.

But for now, as he stands on the threshold of greatness, Hanuman ji knows only one thing—that his quest has only just begun, and that the adventure that awaits him will be the greatest of his life.

The Veil of Destiny

In the celestial realm, where the stars shine with ethereal brilliance and the heavens resound with the hymns of divine beings, the mystery of Hanuman ji's birth continues to unfold—a mystery wrapped in the veils of destiny and woven into the fabric of time itself.

As Hanuman ji delves deeper into his quest for knowledge, he finds himself drawn into the labyrinthine corridors of fate—a realm where the past, present, and future converge in a kaleidoscope of cosmic patterns and celestial designs.

Driven by an insatiable curiosity and an unyielding determination, Hanuman ji presses on, his heart ablaze with the fire of righteous purpose and his spirit fortified by the wisdom of his divine heritage. With each step he takes, he draws closer to the truth, closer to the realization of his true potential, and closer to the destiny that awaits him.

But the path ahead is fraught with peril, for the veils of destiny are not easily pierced, and the secrets they conceal are guarded by forces beyond mortal comprehension. Undeterred by the challenges that lie ahead, Hanuman ji presses on, his resolve unshaken and his faith unwavering.

As he navigates the treacherous currents of fate, Hanuman ji encounters beings both celestial and infernal, each offering cryptic clues to the mystery of his birth. From ancient sages to powerful deities, from malevolent demons to benevolent spirits, each encounter brings him closer to the truth, and each challenge strengthens his resolve.

But amidst the trials and tribulations of his journey, Hanuman ji remains steadfast in his quest, guided by the wisdom of his divine heritage and the teachings of his beloved mother Anjana. With her words echoing in his ears and her love burning in his heart, Hanuman ji presses on, his faith unshakable and his spirit unyielding.

And so, as the days turn into weeks and the weeks into months, Hanuman ji's quest for knowledge becomes a journey of self-discovery—a journey that will not only reveal the truth of his origins, but also forge him into the greatest hero the world has ever known.

For in the heart of every hero lies the fire of righteous purpose, the flame of divine guidance, and the strength of unwavering determination. And as Hanuman ji continues on his quest, he knows that with each step he takes, he draws closer to the destiny that awaits him, closer to the truth of his existence, and closer to the realization of his true potential.

But for now, as he stands on the threshold of greatness, Hanuman ji knows only one thing—that his quest has only just begun, and that the adventure that awaits him will be the greatest of his life.

The Revelations Unveiled

As Hanuman ji delves deeper into the labyrinth of fate, he finds himself standing on the precipice of revelation—a realm where the veils of mystery are lifted, and the truths of his existence are laid bare before him.

Driven by an insatiable thirst for knowledge and a burning desire to uncover the secrets of his past, Hanuman ji presses onward, his heart pulsating with anticipation and his spirit aflame with determination. With each step he takes, he feels the weight of destiny upon his shoulders, urging him ever forward towards the illumination that awaits.

But the path to enlightenment is fraught with obstacles, for the forces of darkness are relentless in their pursuit of power and deception. Undeterred by the shadows that threaten to engulf him, Hanuman ji summons forth the light of his divine heritage, casting aside the darkness with the radiance of his unwavering faith.

As he traverses the winding corridors of fate, Hanuman ji encounters beings both celestial and infernal, each offering cryptic clues to the mystery of his birth. From ancient sages to powerful deities, from malevolent demons to benevolent spirits, each encounter brings him closer to the truth, and each challenge strengthens his resolve.

But amidst the trials and tribulations of his journey, Hanuman ji remains steadfast in his quest, guided by the wisdom of his divine heritage and the teachings of his beloved mother Anjana. With her words echoing in his ears and her love burning in his heart, Hanuman ji presses on, his faith unshakable and his spirit unyielding.

And so, as the days turn into weeks and the weeks into months, Hanuman ji's quest for knowledge becomes a journey of self-discovery—a journey that will not only reveal the truth of his origins, but also forge him into the greatest hero the world has ever known.

For in the heart of every hero lies the fire of righteous purpose, the flame of divine guidance, and the strength of unwavering determination. And as Hanuman ji continues on his quest, he knows that with each step he takes, he draws closer to the destiny that awaits him, closer to the truth of his existence, and closer to the realization of his true potential.

But for now, as he stands on the threshold of greatness, Hanuman ji knows only one thing—that his quest has only just begun, and that the adventure that awaits him will be the greatest of his life.

The Final Revelation

As Hanuman ji ventures deeper into the heart of destiny's labyrinth, he senses a shift in the cosmic currents—a subtle whisper of revelation, beckoning him towards the ultimate truth that lies at the core of his existence.

Driven by an unwavering resolve and a relentless thirst for knowledge, Hanuman ji presses on, his heart ablaze with the fire of righteous purpose and his spirit fortified by the wisdom of his divine heritage. With each step he takes, he feels the weight of destiny upon his shoulders, urging him ever forward towards the culmination of his quest.

But the path to enlightenment is fraught with peril, for the forces of darkness are arrayed against him, seeking to thwart his every move and obscure the truth that lies beyond. Undeterred by the shadows that threaten to engulf him, Hanuman ji summons forth the light of his divine essence, banishing the darkness with the radiance of his unwavering faith.

As he navigates the treacherous twists and turns of fate, Hanuman ji encounters beings both celestial and infernal, each offering cryptic clues to the mystery of his birth. From ancient sages to powerful deities, from malevolent demons to benevolent spirits, each encounter brings him closer to the truth, and each challenge strengthens his resolve.

But amidst the trials and tribulations of his journey, Hanuman ji remains steadfast in his quest, guided by the wisdom of his divine heritage and the teachings of his beloved mother Anjana. With her words echoing in his ears and her love burning in his heart, Hanuman ji presses on, his faith unshakable and his spirit unyielding.

And so, as the days turn into weeks and the weeks into months, Hanuman ji's quest for knowledge becomes a journey of self-discovery—a journey that will not only reveal the truth of his origins, but also forge him into the greatest hero the world has ever known.

For in the heart of every hero lies the fire of righteous purpose, the flame of divine guidance, and the strength of unwavering determination. And as Hanuman ji continues on his quest, he knows that with each step he takes, he draws closer to the destiny that awaits him, closer to the truth of his existence, and closer to the realization of his true potential.

But for now, as he stands on the threshold of greatness, Hanuman ji knows only one thing—that his quest has only just begun, and that the adventure that awaits him will be the greatest of his life.

Hanuman ji Devotion to Lord Rama

The Divine Encounter

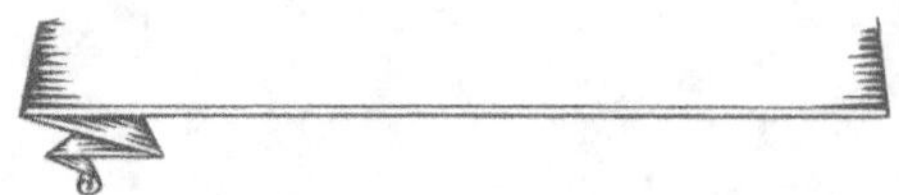

In the sacred forests of Dandakaranya, where the ancient trees whisper secrets of forgotten truths and the rivers sing songs of celestial praise, a divine encounter unfolds—a meeting that will forever alter the course of history and bind two souls in an unbreakable bond of love and devotion.

It is here, amidst the lush foliage and tranquil serenity of the forest, that Hanuman ji first sets eyes upon Lord Rama—a sight that fills his heart with a sense of awe and reverence, and ignites within him a flame of devotion that will burn brightly for all eternity.

As he stands before Rama, his heart pounding with excitement and his eyes shining with reverence, Hanuman ji feels a surge of emotion unlike anything he has ever experienced before. For in Rama, he sees not just a prince, but a divine incarnation—a manifestation of dharma and righteousness, whose very presence fills the air with an aura of divine grace.

In that moment, Hanuman ji knows that his destiny is irrevocably entwined with that of Rama, and that he will follow his lord to the ends of the earth and beyond. Drawn to Rama by an unbreakable bond of love and devotion, Hanuman ji offers himself as a humble servant, ready to fulfill whatever task his lord may require of him.

And so, as Rama gazes upon Hanuman ji with eyes filled with compassion and love, he extends his hand in friendship, sealing the bond between them for all eternity. In that moment, the world fades away, and there is only Hanuman ji and Rama, bound together by the ties of love and devotion that transcend mortal understanding.

As they embark on their journey together, Hanuman ji's devotion to Rama knows no bounds, his love for his lord shining like a beacon of light in the darkness. Whether battling demons on the battlefield or facing the trials of exile, Hanuman ji remains steadfast in his devotion, his unwavering faith serving as a source of strength and inspiration for all who follow him.

And so, as they traverse the length and breadth of the earth, Hanuman ji and Rama become not just master and servant, but brothers in arms, united in their quest for righteousness and justice. For in the heart of every devotee beats the spirit of Hanuman ji—a spirit that knows no fear, no doubt, and no defeat, but only the boundless love and devotion for his beloved lord.

The Journey Begins

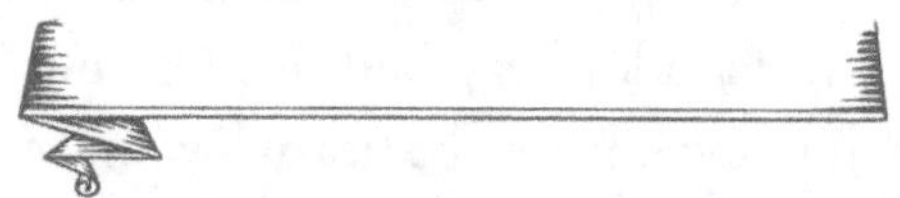

With the bond between Hanuman ji and Lord Rama sealed in the sacred forests of Dandakaranya, their journey together begins—a journey marked by trials and triumphs, challenges and victories, but above all, by the unbreakable bond of love and devotion that binds them together.

As they traverse the vast expanse of the forest, Hanuman ji's devotion to Lord Rama shines like a guiding star in the night sky, lighting their path and illuminating the darkness that surrounds them. With each step they take, their bond grows stronger, their spirits intertwined in a dance of divine love and cosmic harmony.

But their journey is not without its challenges, for the forests of Dandakaranya are teeming with dangers and obstacles that test their resolve and challenge their faith. From ferocious demons to treacherous terrain, from malevolent spirits to insurmountable odds, Hanuman ji and Lord Rama face each trial together, their devotion serving as a shield against the forces of darkness that seek to thwart their quest.

And yet, amidst the trials and tribulations of their journey, there are also moments of joy and celebration—moments when Hanuman ji's devotion shines brightest, illuminating the path ahead and guiding them towards their ultimate destination. Whether battling demons on the battlefield or sharing moments of camaraderie around the campfire, Hanuman ji's unwavering love for his lord is a constant source of strength and inspiration for all who follow him.

And so, as they continue on their journey together, Hanuman ji and Lord Rama become not just master and servant, but brothers in arms, united in their quest for righteousness and justice. For in the heart of every devotee beats the spirit of Hanuman ji—a spirit that knows no fear, no doubt, and no defeat, but only the boundless love and devotion for his beloved lord.

The Test of Devotion

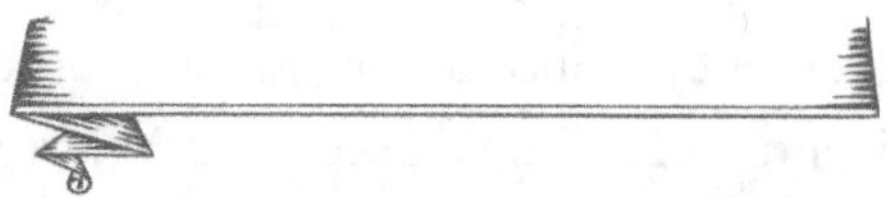

As Hanuman ji and Lord Rama journey through the forests of Dandakaranya, their bond of devotion is put to the ultimate test—a test that will push them to the limits of their faith and endurance, but ultimately strengthen the unbreakable bond that binds them together.

Amidst the dense foliage and towering trees, they encounter a series of challenges that threaten to shake their resolve and test the depth of their devotion. From cunning demons to devious traps, from treacherous terrain to unforeseen obstacles, Hanuman ji and Lord Rama face each trial with unwavering determination and unyielding faith.

But it is not just the external challenges that test their devotion—it is also the internal struggles that threaten to undermine their faith and weaken their resolve. As doubts and fears creep into their minds, Hanuman ji and Lord Rama must confront the shadows within themselves, and find the strength to overcome the darkness that threatens to engulf them.

In these moments of trial and tribulation, Hanuman ji's devotion shines brightest, serving as a beacon of light in the darkest of times. With each challenge they overcome, their bond grows stronger, their spirits intertwined in a dance of divine love and cosmic harmony.

And so, as they press on through the forests of Dandakaranya, Hanuman ji and Lord Rama emerge victorious, their devotion unshaken and their bond unbreakable. For in the heart of every devotee beats the spirit of Hanuman ji—a spirit that knows no fear, no doubt, and no defeat, but only the boundless love and devotion for his beloved lord.

The Sacrifice of Devotion

In the heart of the forest, amidst the whispers of the ancient trees and the gentle rustle of the leaves, Hanuman ji's devotion to Lord Rama is put to the ultimate test—a test that demands the ultimate sacrifice, but ultimately reaffirms the unbreakable bond between devotee and lord.

As they journey through the dense undergrowth, Hanuman ji and Lord Rama come face to face with a formidable obstacle—a towering mountain that blocks their path and threatens to halt their progress. Undeterred by the seemingly insurmountable barrier, Hanuman ji resolves to find a way forward, his heart ablaze with the fire of devotion and his spirit fortified by the strength of his faith.

But as he surveys the towering peak before him, Hanuman ji realizes that the only way to overcome this obstacle is through sacrifice—a sacrifice that will test the limits of his devotion and challenge the very essence of his being. With a heavy heart and a determined spirit, Hanuman ji prepares to make the ultimate sacrifice, offering himself as a willing sacrifice to clear the path for his beloved lord.

With a mighty roar that shakes the very foundations of the earth, Hanuman ji hurls himself towards the towering peak, his body transformed into a living missile of divine power and celestial grace. As he crashes into the mountain with the force of a thousand thunderbolts, the earth trembles and the skies darken, but Hanuman ji does not falter, his devotion unwavering and his sacrifice unmatched in its purity and selflessness.

And so, as the dust settles and the mountain crumbles to dust, Hanuman ji emerges victorious, his sacrifice paving the way for Lord Rama and his companions to continue on their journey. For in the heart of every devotee beats the spirit of Hanuman ji—a spirit that knows no fear, no doubt, and no defeat, but only the boundless love and devotion for his beloved lord.

The Triumph of Devotion

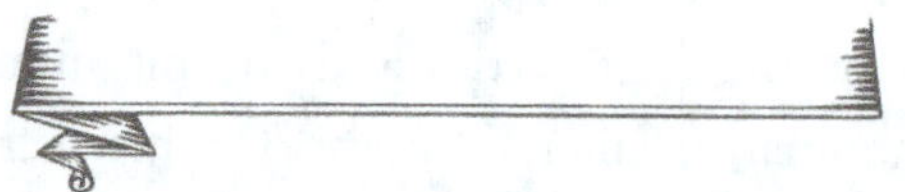

As the echoes of Hanuman ji's sacrifice reverberate through the forest, a sense of awe and reverence fills the air—a testament to the power of devotion and the triumph of righteousness that shines brightly in the hearts of all who witness this divine spectacle.

With the mountainous obstacle cleared from their path, Hanuman ji and Lord Rama continue their journey through the forests of Dandakaranya, their spirits uplifted and their resolve strengthened by the selfless act of devotion that has paved the way for their progress.

But the true triumph of devotion is not measured in feats of strength or acts of valor—it is measured in the purity of the heart and the depth of the soul, in the unwavering faith that guides one through the darkest of times and the fiercest of trials.

As Hanuman ji and Lord Rama press on towards their ultimate destination, their bond of devotion grows stronger with each passing moment, their spirits intertwined in a dance of divine love and cosmic harmony. For in the heart of every devotee beats the spirit of Hanuman ji—a spirit that knows no fear, no doubt, and no defeat, but only the boundless love and devotion for his beloved lord.

And so, as they journey through the forests of Dandakaranya, Hanuman ji and Lord Rama become not just master and servant, but brothers in arms, united in their quest for righteousness and justice. For in the heart of every devotee beats the spirit of Hanuman ji—a spirit that knows no fear, no doubt, and no defeat, but only the boundless love and devotion for his beloved lord.

The Eternal Bond

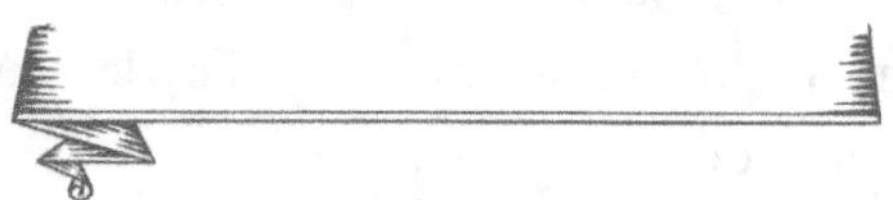

As Hanuman ji and Lord Rama emerge from the forests of Dandakaranya, their journey together reaches its culmination—a journey marked by trials and triumphs, challenges and victories, but above all, by the unbreakable bond of love and devotion that binds them together for all eternity.

With each step they take, their bond grows stronger, their spirits intertwined in a dance of divine love and cosmic harmony. For in the heart of every devotee beats the spirit of Hanuman ji—a spirit that knows no fear, no doubt, and no defeat, but only the boundless love and devotion for his beloved lord.

As they stand side by side, gazing out over the horizon, Hanuman ji and Lord Rama know that their journey together is far from over. For in the heart of every devotee beats the spirit of Hanuman ji—a spirit that knows no fear, no doubt, and no defeat, but only the boundless love and devotion for his beloved lord.

And so, as they embark on the next chapter of their journey together, Hanuman ji and Lord Rama know that their bond of love and devotion will carry them through whatever challenges lie ahead. For in the heart of every devotee beats the spirit of Hanuman ji—a spirit that knows no fear, no doubt, and no defeat, but only the boundless love and devotion for his beloved lord.

Hanuman ji Power and Abilities

Hanuman Ji: The Epitome of Courage and Valor

In the annals of mythology and legend, there exists a figure whose name resounds with tales of boundless courage and indomitable valor—a figure whose deeds inspire awe and admiration in the hearts of all who hear his story. This is the tale of Hanuman Ji, the mighty monkey god whose powers and abilities are as vast and boundless as the heavens themselves.

Born to the celestial nymph Anjana and the wind god Vayu, Hanuman Ji entered the world with a sense of purpose and destiny that set him apart from all others. From his earliest days, he displayed signs of his extraordinary powers, performing feats of strength and valor that astounded even the mightiest of beings.

But it was not just his physical prowess that made Hanuman Ji a figure of legend—it was also his unwavering courage and fearless determination in the face of adversity. From battling fearsome demons to traversing treacherous landscapes, Hanuman Ji faced each challenge with a bravery and resolve that knew no equal, his spirit unyielding and his heart unshakable.

As he journeyed through the world, Hanuman Ji's courage and valor were put to the test time and time again, as he faced enemies both mortal and divine, each more formidable than the last. But with each trial he faced, Hanuman Ji emerged victorious, his bravery shining like a beacon in the darkness, guiding him ever forward on his path.

But perhaps the true measure of Hanuman Ji's courage and valor lay not in his victories on the battlefield, but in his unwavering devotion to his beloved lord, Lord Rama. For it was this devotion that fueled his every action, driving him to perform acts of heroism and selflessness that would echo through the ages.

And so, as we embark on this journey through the life and legend of Hanuman Ji, let us remember the courage and valor that define his character, and let us draw inspiration from his unwavering devotion to duty and righteousness.

The Divine Origins Unveiled

In the celestial realm, where the stars dance in eternal harmony and the gods weave the threads of destiny, the tale of Hanuman Ji's divine origins unfolds—a story shrouded in mystery and steeped in myth, yet imbued with a sense of timeless wonder and celestial grace.

Hanuman Ji, the mighty monkey god, was not born of mortal flesh and blood, but of celestial lineage, descended from the heavens themselves. His mother, Anjana, was a celestial nymph of unparalleled beauty and grace, while his father, Vayu, was the wind god whose breath gave life to the world.

From the moment of his conception, Hanuman Ji was destined for greatness, his every step guided by the hand of destiny and the wisdom of the gods. As he emerged into the world, his radiant form illuminated the heavens, filling all who beheld him with a sense of awe and wonder.

But it was not just his divine lineage that set Hanuman Ji apart—it was also his extraordinary powers and abilities, which surpassed those of mortal and celestial alike. From his incredible strength to his unmatched agility, Hanuman Ji possessed powers that defied mortal understanding, his every action a testament to the boundless potential of the divine.

As he grew from infancy to adolescence, Hanuman Ji's powers only continued to grow, his every deed a reflection of his divine heritage and celestial grace. From performing miraculous feats of strength to outwitting the most cunning of adversaries, Hanuman Ji's legend grew with each passing day, his name whispered in hushed tones by gods and mortals alike.

But amidst the wonder and splendor of his divine origins, there was also a sense of destiny—a destiny that would lead Hanuman Ji down a path of heroism and sacrifice, of courage and valor, and ultimately, of divine enlightenment.

And so, as we marvel at the tale of Hanuman Ji's divine origins, let us remember the timeless wisdom that lies at the heart of his story—that true greatness lies not in the powers we possess, but in the deeds we perform and the lives we touch along the way.

The Divine Childhood: Nurturing the Seed of Greatness

In the celestial realm, where the essence of divinity permeates every corner and the air is filled with the whispers of ancient wisdom, Hanuman Ji spent his formative years cradled in the embrace of celestial love and guided by the hand of destiny. This is the story of his divine childhood—a time of innocence and wonder, marked by the nurturing of a seed of greatness destined to bloom into a legend for the ages.

Born of the celestial nymph Anjana and the wind god Vayu, Hanuman Ji entered the world with a brilliance that illuminated the heavens, his radiant form a beacon of hope and promise for all who beheld him. From the moment of his birth, he was enveloped in the love and adoration of his celestial parents, their divine presence shaping his every thought and action.

As Hanuman Ji grew from infancy to childhood, his days were filled with the joyous laughter of celestial beings and the gentle caress of the celestial winds. Surrounded by the beauty of the celestial gardens and the splendor of the celestial court, he roamed freely, his boundless curiosity leading him to explore every corner of his celestial home.

But amidst the wonder and splendor of his divine surroundings, there was also a sense of destiny—a destiny that would call him to a life of heroism and sacrifice, of courage and valor, and ultimately, of divine enlightenment. From his earliest days, Hanuman Ji displayed signs of his extraordinary powers, performing miraculous feats of strength and agility that astounded all who witnessed them.

But it was not just his physical prowess that set Hanuman Ji apart—it was also his unwavering devotion to duty and righteousness, his every action a reflection of his divine heritage and celestial grace. From assisting the celestial sages in their quest for knowledge to protecting the innocent from harm, Hanuman Ji's compassion and selflessness knew no bounds, his heart overflowing with love for all beings.

And so, as Hanuman Ji's divine childhood unfolded amidst the splendor of the celestial realm, he grew into a figure of legend and wonder, his every action guided by the hand of destiny and the wisdom of the gods. And though his journey had only just begun, the seeds of greatness had already been planted, destined to blossom into the mighty tree of heroism and sacrifice that would define his legacy for all eternity.

The Mentor's Wisdom

In the celestial realm, where the stars illuminate the path of destiny and the gods weave the threads of fate, Hanuman Ji's divine childhood was further enriched by the guidance and wisdom of his celestial mentors. Among these revered beings was the sage Narada, whose boundless knowledge and sage advice would shape the course of Hanuman Ji's life and instill within him the virtues of wisdom and righteousness.

From a young age, Hanuman Ji was drawn to the presence of Narada, whose aura radiated with the brilliance of a thousand suns and whose wisdom transcended the boundaries of mortal understanding. Under Narada's tutelage, Hanuman Ji embarked on a journey of self-discovery and enlightenment, delving deep into the mysteries of the universe and uncovering the secrets of his own divine nature.

As they wandered through the celestial realms, Narada shared with Hanuman Ji the timeless wisdom of the sages, imparting upon him the knowledge of the ages and guiding him along the path of righteousness. From the sacred scriptures to the sacred mantras, from the ancient hymns to the celestial chants, Narada opened the doors of knowledge to Hanuman Ji, allowing him to drink deeply from the wellspring of divine wisdom.

But perhaps the greatest lesson that Narada imparted upon Hanuman Ji was the importance of humility and selflessness in the pursuit of greatness. For Narada knew that true wisdom lay not in the accumulation of knowledge, but in the application of that knowledge for the greater good of all beings.

And so, as Hanuman Ji's divine childhood unfolded under the watchful eye of his celestial mentor, he grew not only in strength and power, but also in wisdom and virtue. With each passing day, he became more attuned to the rhythms of the universe and more aligned with the will of the gods, his every action guided by the timeless wisdom of the sage Narada.

And though his journey had only just begun, Hanuman Ji knew that with Narada's guidance and wisdom lighting his way, he would be ready to face whatever challenges lay ahead, armed with the knowledge and virtue to overcome any obstacle in his path.

The Trials of Growth

As Hanuman Ji's divine childhood progressed, so too did the trials and tribulations that tested his courage, strength, and wisdom. Amidst the serene beauty of the celestial realm, he faced challenges that would shape him into the mighty hero and divine being he was destined to become.

One such trial came in the form of a confrontation with the fearsome demon Kalanemi, whose dark presence threatened to unleash chaos and destruction upon the celestial realms. Sensing the impending danger, Hanuman Ji rose to the challenge, his heart ablaze with courage and determination.

With Narada's wisdom guiding him and the blessings of the gods upon him, Hanuman Ji confronted Kalanemi in a fierce battle that shook the heavens themselves. With each blow exchanged, Hanuman Ji's strength and valor were put to the test, his every move a testament to his unwavering commitment to protect the celestial realm from harm.

But it was not just physical strength that Hanuman Ji relied upon in his battle against Kalanemi—it was also his wisdom and cunning, his ability to outmaneuver his opponent and anticipate his every move. With Narada's teachings echoing in his mind, Hanuman Ji exploited Kalanemi's weaknesses and turned the tide of battle in his favor, emerging victorious against all odds.

Yet, the trials of growth did not end with the defeat of Kalanemi, for Hanuman Ji knew that true greatness lay not in the triumph of the body, but in the triumph of the spirit. And so, he continued to face each challenge with humility and determination, his every victory tempered by the knowledge that there was still much to learn and much to overcome.

And so, as Hanuman Ji's divine childhood drew to a close, he emerged stronger, wiser, and more determined than ever before. With Narada's guidance lighting his way, he knew that the trials he faced were but stepping stones on the path to his ultimate destiny—a destiny that would see him become the greatest hero the world had ever known.

The Dawn of Destiny

As Hanuman Ji's divine childhood came to an end, the dawn of destiny beckoned, calling him forth to fulfill his sacred purpose and embark on a journey that would forever alter the course of history. With Narada's wisdom echoing in his heart and the blessings of the gods upon him, Hanuman Ji stood ready to face whatever challenges lay ahead, armed with the courage, strength, and wisdom of a true hero.

But before he could embark on his destined path, Hanuman Ji received one final lesson from his celestial mentor—a lesson that would serve as the foundation upon which his future endeavors would be built. Narada spoke of the importance of service and sacrifice, of putting the needs of others before one's own and dedicating one's life to the greater good of all beings.

With these words ringing in his ears, Hanuman Ji bowed before Narada, his heart filled with gratitude and reverence for the wisdom and guidance he had received. And as he set forth on his journey, he carried with him the lessons of his divine childhood, a beacon of light to illuminate the path ahead.

With each step he took, Hanuman Ji's legend grew, his name whispered in hushed tones by gods and mortals alike. From the celestial realms to the mortal world below, his deeds of valor and heroism echoed through the ages, inspiring all who heard his story to strive for greatness and live a life of courage, strength, and virtue.

And though his journey would be fraught with trials and tribulations, Hanuman Ji faced each challenge with unwavering determination and unyielding resolve, his spirit undimmed by the darkness that surrounded him. For he knew that with Narada's wisdom guiding him and the blessings of the gods upon him, he was destined for greatness—a destiny that would see him become the greatest hero the world had ever known.

And so, as Hanuman Ji's divine childhood faded into memory, he embraced the dawn of destiny with open arms, ready to face whatever challenges lay ahead and fulfill his sacred purpose with courage, strength, and unwavering devotion.

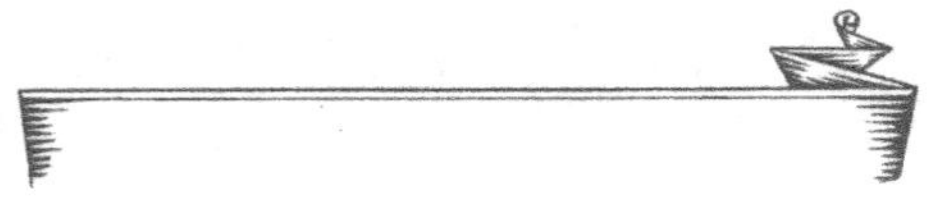

Hanuman Ji's role in the Ramayana

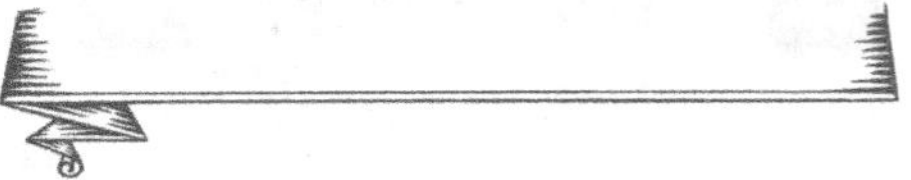

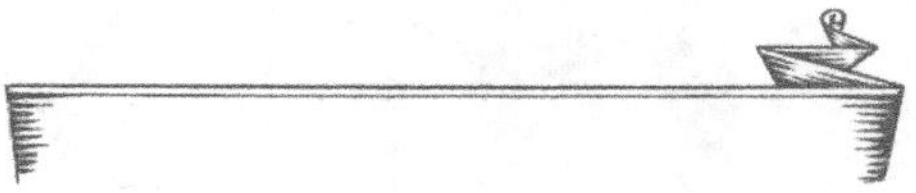

Hanuman Ji's Heroic Journey in the Ramayana

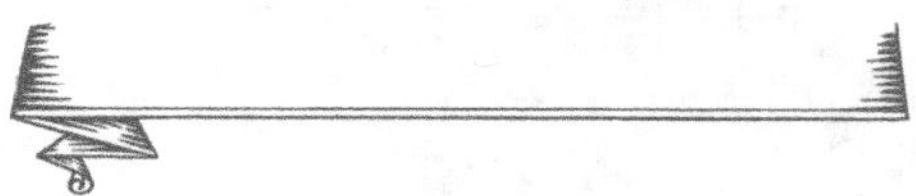

In the ancient epic of the Ramayana, Hanuman Ji emerges as a central figure whose heroic deeds and unwavering devotion play a pivotal role in the unfolding of the divine drama. From his humble beginnings to his awe-inspiring feats of strength and courage, Hanuman Ji's journey in the Ramayana is a testament to the power of faith, loyalty, and selflessness.

The Ramayana begins with the story of Prince Rama, the beloved son of King Dasharatha of Ayodhya, who is unjustly exiled from his kingdom and forced to wander the wilderness with his devoted wife, Sita, and loyal brother, Lakshmana. As they journey through the forests of India, they encounter various challenges and adversaries, including the demon king Ravana, whose nefarious deeds threaten to plunge the world into darkness.

It is in this tumultuous time that Hanuman Ji enters the stage, summoned by the gods to aid Prince Rama in his quest to rescue Sita and defeat the forces of evil. Descending from the heavens in a blaze of divine glory, Hanuman Ji assumes the form of a humble monkey and sets forth on his mission with unwavering determination and boundless courage.

As Hanuman Ji traverses the length and breadth of the Indian subcontinent, his every action is guided by the hand of destiny and the wisdom of the gods. From battling demons on the battlefield to outwitting the most cunning of adversaries, Hanuman Ji's legend grows with each passing day, his name whispered in awe and admiration by gods and mortals alike.

But perhaps the most iconic moment in Hanuman Ji's journey comes when he encounters Sita, who has been abducted by Ravana and imprisoned in his fortress in Lanka. In a display of unparalleled devotion and selflessness, Hanuman Ji crosses the vast ocean to reach Lanka, his every leap spanning leagues in a single bound.

Upon reaching Lanka, Hanuman Ji assumes a diminutive form and infiltrates the fortress, using his cunning and agility to evade detection and locate Sita. When he finally finds her, he delivers Prince Rama's message of love and reassurance, restoring hope to her heart and filling her with renewed strength and resolve.

But Hanuman Ji's mission is far from over, for he must now return to Prince Rama and deliver the news of Sita's whereabouts, thus setting in motion the events that will ultimately lead to the epic battle between good and evil. And so, with his divine mission fulfilled, Hanuman Ji prepares to return to his beloved lord, his heart filled with devotion and his spirit ablaze with the fire of righteousness.

As we embark on this journey through the Ramayana, let us remember the heroic deeds of Hanuman Ji and the pivotal role he plays in the divine drama. For in his unwavering devotion and boundless courage, we find inspiration to face our own challenges with strength, courage, and unwavering faith.

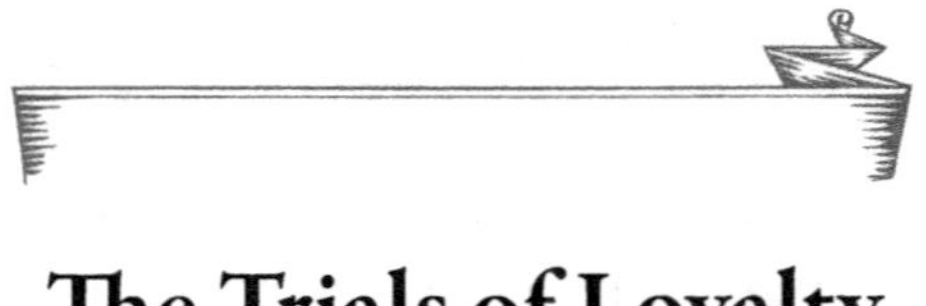

The Trials of Loyalty

As Hanuman Ji's journey in the Ramayana unfolds, he finds himself confronted with a series of trials that test not only his physical prowess but also the depth of his loyalty and devotion to Prince Rama. From the moment he sets foot in Lanka to the final battle against the forces of evil, Hanuman Ji's unwavering commitment to his beloved lord shines brightly, guiding him through the darkest of times and inspiring all who witness his heroic deeds.

In the fortress of Lanka, Hanuman Ji faces his first trial of loyalty as he searches for Sita amidst the enemy stronghold. Despite the countless obstacles and dangers that lie in his path, he remains steadfast in his resolve, his every action guided by the knowledge that he is serving a higher purpose—a purpose that transcends mortal concerns and embodies the very essence of divine duty.

But it is not just physical obstacles that Hanuman Ji must overcome—it is also the doubts and fears that threaten to undermine his faith and weaken his resolve. As he navigates the treacherous corridors of the fortress and confronts the demons that guard its halls, Hanuman Ji draws strength from the memory of Prince Rama and the love they share, knowing that his loyalty to his beloved lord will see him through even the darkest of times.

As he finally locates Sita amidst the ruins of the fortress, Hanuman Ji is filled with a sense of triumph and relief, his heart swelling with pride at the sight of her radiant beauty. But his joy is short-lived, for he knows that his mission is far from over—he must now return to Prince Rama and deliver the news of Sita's whereabouts, thus setting in motion the events that will ultimately lead to the epic battle between good and evil.

And so, with his heart filled with determination and his spirit ablaze with the fire of righteousness, Hanuman Ji prepares to face the trials that lie ahead, knowing that his loyalty to Prince Rama will see him through whatever challenges may come his way. For in the heart of every devotee beats the spirit of Hanuman Ji—a spirit that knows no fear, no doubt, and no defeat, but only the boundless love and devotion for his beloved lord.

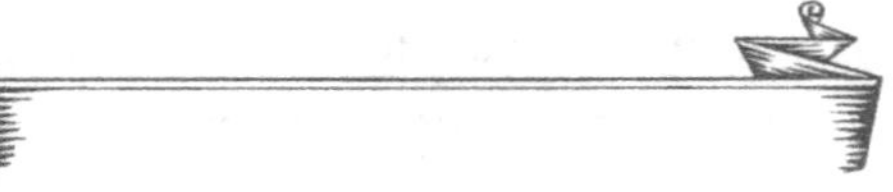

The Courage to Serve

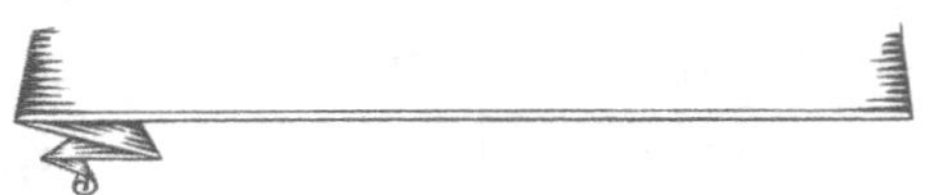

As Hanuman Ji's journey in the Ramayana continues, he exemplifies the virtue of courage in the face of daunting challenges, demonstrating unwavering resolve and selflessness in his service to Prince Rama and the cause of righteousness. From his daring exploits on the battlefield to his unwavering devotion to his beloved lord, Hanuman Ji's courage shines brightly, inspiring all who witness his heroic deeds.

One of the most iconic moments in Hanuman Ji's journey is his leap across the ocean to reach Lanka, where Sita is held captive by the demon king Ravana. With the fate of the world hanging in the balance, Hanuman Ji embarks on this perilous journey with unwavering determination and boundless courage, his every leap spanning leagues in a single bound.

As he soars through the air, the ocean's waves crashing beneath him and the wind howling in his ears, Hanuman Ji's courage is put to the test like never before. But he does not waver, his heart filled with love for his beloved lord and his spirit ablaze with the fire of righteousness.

Upon reaching Lanka, Hanuman Ji faces a series of trials that would daunt even the bravest of souls. From battling demons in the streets to navigating the treacherous corridors of the fortress, he confronts each challenge with unwavering resolve and unyielding courage, his every action guided by the knowledge that he serves a higher purpose—a purpose that transcends mortal concerns and embodies the very essence of divine duty.

But perhaps the truest test of Hanuman Ji's courage comes when he finally locates Sita amidst the ruins of the fortress. Confronted with the sight of her sorrow and despair, he must find the strength to deliver Prince Rama's message of love and reassurance, knowing that the fate of the world hangs in the balance.

With a heart filled with compassion and a spirit imbued with courage, Hanuman Ji delivers Prince Rama's message to Sita, restoring hope to her heart and filling her with renewed strength and resolve. And though his mission is far from over, Hanuman Ji knows that with courage and determination, he will overcome whatever challenges lie ahead, serving his beloved lord with unwavering devotion until the very end.

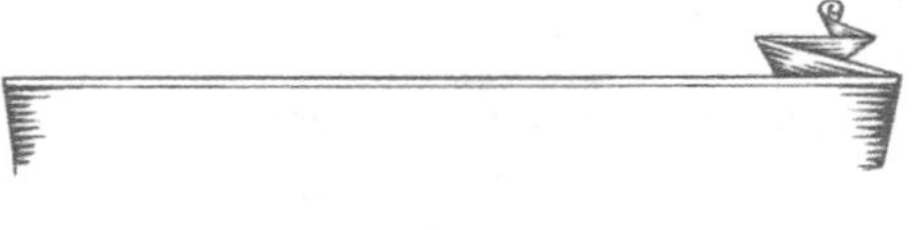

The Sacrifice of Self

In the epic tale of the Ramayana, Hanuman Ji emerges as a towering figure whose unwavering devotion and selfless sacrifice play a central role in the divine drama unfolding before the eyes of gods and mortals alike. His journey is one marked by trials and tribulations, challenges and triumphs, but above all, by the enduring spirit of sacrifice that defines his character and inspires all who witness his heroic deeds.

As Hanuman Ji embarks on his mission to locate Sita, who has been abducted by the demon king Ravana and imprisoned in his fortress in Lanka, he knows that the road ahead will be fraught with danger and uncertainty. But he does not hesitate, for his heart is filled with love for his beloved lord Prince Rama and his spirit ablaze with the fire of righteousness.

As he traverses the vast expanse of the ocean, his every leap spanning leagues in a single bound, Hanuman Ji's courage is put to the test like never before. But he does not waver, for he knows that his mission is one of utmost importance—a mission that transcends mortal concerns and embodies the very essence of divine duty.

Upon reaching Lanka, Hanuman Ji faces a series of trials that would daunt even the bravest of souls. From battling demons in the streets to navigating the treacherous corridors of the fortress, he confronts each challenge with unwavering resolve and unyielding courage, his every action guided by the knowledge that he serves a higher purpose—a purpose that transcends mortal concerns and embodies the very essence of divine duty.

But perhaps the truest test of Hanuman Ji's courage comes when he finally locates Sita amidst the ruins of the fortress. Confronted with the sight of her sorrow and despair, he must find the strength to deliver Prince Rama's message of love and reassurance, knowing that the fate of the world hangs in the balance.

With a heart filled with compassion and a spirit imbued with courage, Hanuman Ji delivers Prince Rama's message to Sita, restoring hope to her heart and filling her with renewed strength and resolve. And though his mission is far from over, Hanuman Ji knows that with courage and determination, he will overcome whatever challenges lie ahead, serving his beloved lord with unwavering devotion until the very end.

But Hanuman Ji's sacrifice does not end with his mission to Lanka, for he knows that true sacrifice requires more than just physical courage—it requires the willingness to endure unimaginable hardships for the sake of others. And so, as the epic battle between good and evil unfolds, Hanuman Ji finds himself at the forefront of the conflict, his every action guided by the knowledge that he serves a higher purpose—a purpose that transcends mortal concerns and embodies the very essence of divine duty.

As he faces the forces of evil on the battlefield, Hanuman Ji knows that victory is not guaranteed, and that he may be called upon to make the ultimate sacrifice for the sake of his beloved lord and the greater good of all beings. But he does not falter, for his heart is filled with love for his beloved lord and his spirit ablaze with the fire of righteousness.

And so, as the battle reaches its climax and the forces of good emerge victorious, Hanuman Ji stands tall amidst the wreckage of war, his sacrifice a testament to the power of love, loyalty, and unwavering devotion. For in the heart of every devotee beats the spirit of Hanuman Ji—a spirit that knows no fear, no doubt, and no defeat, but only the boundless love and devotion for his beloved lord.

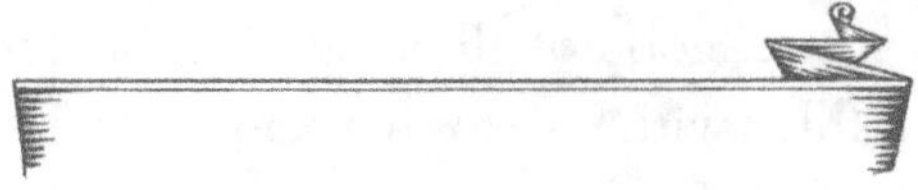

The Triumph of Virtue

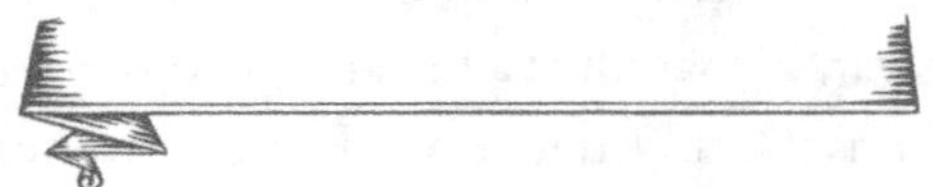

As Hanuman Ji's journey in the Ramayana reaches its climax, he emerges as a symbol of virtue and righteousness, embodying the highest ideals of courage, loyalty, and selflessness. Through his unwavering devotion to his beloved lord Prince Rama and his relentless pursuit of justice and righteousness, Hanuman Ji inspires all who witness his heroic deeds to strive for greatness and live a life of virtue and integrity.

As the epic battle between good and evil reaches its crescendo, Hanuman Ji stands at the forefront of the conflict, his every action guided by the knowledge that he serves a higher purpose—a purpose that transcends mortal concerns and embodies the very essence of divine duty. With courage and determination, he leads the forces of good into battle, his spirit ablaze with the fire of righteousness and his heart filled with love for his beloved lord.

But victory does not come easily, for the forces of evil are formidable and relentless in their pursuit of power and domination. As the battle rages on, Hanuman Ji faces countless adversaries, each more formidable than the last, but he does not falter, for he knows that his cause is just and his purpose noble.

With unwavering resolve and unyielding courage, Hanuman Ji leads the forces of good to victory, his every action a testament to the power of virtue and righteousness. And as the dust settles and the cries of battle fade into the distance, Hanuman Ji stands triumphant amidst the wreckage of war, his sacrifice and valor immortalized in the annals of history.

But Hanuman Ji's journey is far from over, for his quest for righteousness knows no bounds. With the same unwavering devotion and selflessness that guided him through the trials of the Ramayana, he continues to serve his beloved lord Prince Rama and uphold the principles of justice and righteousness wherever he goes.

And though his journey may be fraught with challenges and obstacles, Hanuman Ji knows that with courage, loyalty, and unwavering devotion, he will overcome whatever trials may come his way. For in the heart of every devotee beats the spirit of Hanuman Ji—a spirit that knows no fear, no doubt, and no defeat, but only the boundless love and devotion for his beloved lord.

The Legacy of Hanuman Ji

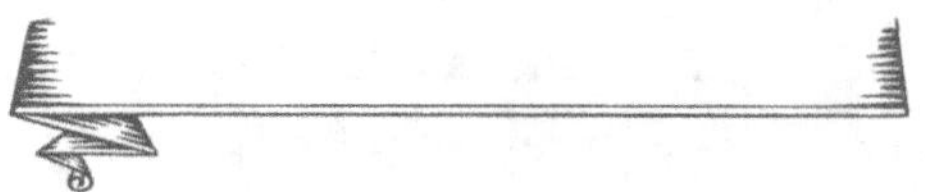

As the epic tale of the Ramayana draws to a close, the legacy of Hanuman Ji lives on, inspiring countless generations with his unwavering devotion, boundless courage, and selfless sacrifice. From his humble beginnings as a divine messenger to his triumphant victory over the forces of evil, Hanuman Ji's journey embodies the highest ideals of virtue and righteousness, serving as a beacon of hope and inspiration for all who seek to follow in his footsteps.

Throughout the ages, Hanuman Ji's legend has been celebrated in song and story, his name whispered in reverence by gods and mortals alike. From the celestial realms to the mortal world below, his heroic deeds are recounted with awe and admiration, inspiring all who hear his tale to strive for greatness and live a life of courage, loyalty, and unwavering devotion.

But perhaps the true legacy of Hanuman Ji lies not in the tales of his heroic exploits, but in the timeless wisdom that he imparts to all who seek his guidance. For in the heart of every devotee beats the spirit of Hanuman Ji—a spirit that knows no fear, no doubt, and no defeat, but only the boundless love and devotion for his beloved lord.

And so, as we reflect on the legacy of Hanuman Ji, let us remember the timeless wisdom that lies at the heart of his story—that true greatness lies not in the powers we possess, but in the deeds we perform and the lives we touch along the way. For in the end, it is not the battles we win or the enemies we defeat that define us, but the love, loyalty, and selflessness that we embody in the service of a greater good.

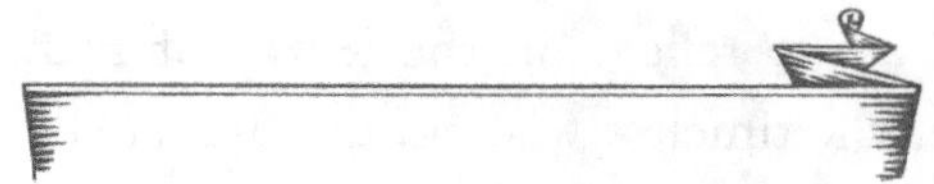

Hanuman Ji's Wisdom and Knowledge

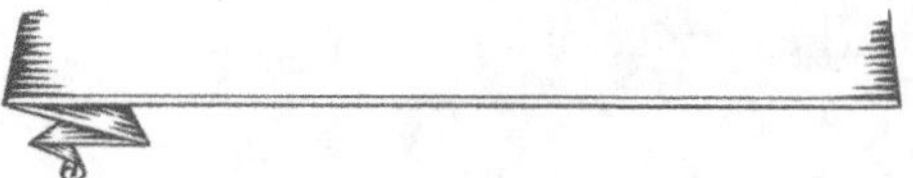

The Wisdom of Hanuman Ji

In the epic tale of the Ramayana, Hanuman Ji emerges not only as a figure of unmatched strength and courage but also as a repository of wisdom and knowledge that transcends mortal understanding. From his early encounters with the sage Narada to his role as a trusted advisor to Prince Rama, Hanuman Ji's wisdom shines brightly, guiding him through the trials and tribulations of his heroic journey and inspiring all who witness his deeds.

From a young age, Hanuman Ji displayed a keen intellect and insatiable thirst for knowledge, eagerly soaking up the teachings of the wise sages and venerable scriptures that surrounded him in the celestial realm. Under the tutelage of the sage Narada, he embarked on a journey of self-discovery and enlightenment, delving deep into the mysteries of the universe and uncovering the secrets of his own divine nature.

But it was not just book knowledge that Hanuman Ji possessed—it was also the wisdom that comes from lived experience and a deep connection to the divine. As he traversed the length and breadth of the Indian subcontinent in search of Sita, he encountered beings of all shapes and sizes, each with their own stories and lessons to impart.

From the humblest peasant to the mightiest warrior, Hanuman Ji listened with an open heart and an attentive mind, absorbing the wisdom of the ages and incorporating it into his own understanding of the world. And as he faced the trials and tribulations of his journey, he drew upon this wisdom time and again, using it to overcome obstacles and navigate the complexities of mortal existence.

But perhaps the truest test of Hanuman Ji's wisdom came when he finally located Sita amidst the ruins of the fortress in Lanka. Confronted with her sorrow and despair, he knew that mere words would not suffice to comfort her—he needed to offer her something more, something that would restore hope to her heart and fill her with renewed strength and resolve.

And so, drawing upon the teachings of the sage Narada and the wisdom of his own experiences, Hanuman Ji spoke words of comfort and reassurance to Sita, reminding her of Prince Rama's unwavering love and devotion and filling her with the knowledge that she was not alone in her suffering.

In the end, it is Hanuman Ji's wisdom that sets him apart from other heroes of the Ramayana—not his physical strength or martial prowess, but his deep understanding of the world and his unwavering commitment to the principles of righteousness and justice. And as we reflect on his story, let us remember the timeless wisdom that he imparts to all who seek his guidance, inspiring us to strive for greatness and live a life of virtue and integrity.

The Journey of Self-Discovery

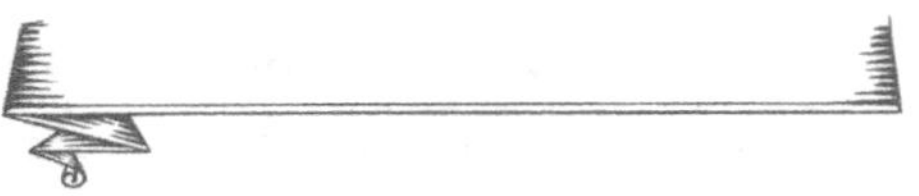

As Hanuman Ji's journey in the Ramayana unfolds, he embarks on a profound journey of self-discovery, delving deep into the depths of his own soul and uncovering the divine wisdom that lies within. From his early encounters with the sage Narada to his transformative experiences on the battlefield and beyond, Hanuman Ji's quest for self-understanding illuminates the path of righteousness for all who seek to follow in his footsteps.

In his youth, Hanuman Ji was blessed with the guidance of the sage Narada, whose boundless knowledge and sage advice would shape the course of his life and instill within him the virtues of wisdom and righteousness. Under Narada's tutelage, Hanuman Ji learned to see beyond the surface of things, delving into the mysteries of the universe and uncovering the secrets of his own divine nature.

But it was not just the teachings of the sage Narada that shaped Hanuman Ji's understanding of the world—it was also his lived experiences and the challenges he faced along his journey. From his encounters with demons and adversaries to his interactions with beings of all shapes and sizes, each moment served as an opportunity for growth and self-discovery, allowing him to delve deeper into the depths of his own soul and uncover the truths that lay hidden within.

As he traversed the length and breadth of the Indian subcontinent in search of Sita, Hanuman Ji confronted the darkness that lurked within himself, wrestling with doubt and uncertainty as he grappled with the enormity of the task before him. But with each trial and tribulation he faced, he emerged stronger and wiser, his understanding of the world deepening with every step he took.

And so, as Hanuman Ji's journey in the Ramayana reaches its climax, he stands as a beacon of wisdom and enlightenment, his every action guided by the knowledge that he serves a higher purpose—a purpose that transcends mortal concerns and embodies the very essence of divine duty. For in the heart of every devotee beats the spirit of Hanuman Ji—a spirit that knows no fear, no doubt, and no defeat, but only the boundless love and devotion for his beloved lord.

The Wisdom of Service

Throughout the epic journey of the Ramayana, Hanuman Ji exemplifies the profound wisdom that comes from selfless service and devotion to a higher cause. As he navigates the trials and tribulations of his heroic quest, Hanuman Ji's unwavering commitment to serving his beloved lord Prince Rama becomes a guiding light for all who seek to walk the path of righteousness and virtue.

From the moment he sets foot in Lanka to the final battle against the forces of evil, Hanuman Ji's every action is driven by his deep sense of duty and devotion to his beloved lord. Despite the countless obstacles and dangers that he faces along the way, he remains steadfast in his resolve, his heart filled with love for Prince Rama and his spirit ablaze with the fire of righteousness.

But it is not just physical strength that Hanuman Ji brings to his service—it is also the wisdom that comes from a life dedicated to the pursuit of truth and justice. As he confronts the darkness that lurks within himself and the world around him, he draws upon the teachings of the sage Narada and the wisdom of his own experiences, using them to guide his actions and illuminate the path of righteousness for all who follow in his footsteps.

One of the most profound lessons that Hanuman Ji imparts through his service is the importance of humility and selflessness. Despite his immense power and divine status, he never seeks glory or recognition for himself, but instead dedicates himself wholeheartedly to the service of his beloved lord and the greater good of all beings.

In his interactions with Sita, Hanuman Ji demonstrates the true meaning of selfless service, comforting her in her darkest hour and offering her hope and reassurance in the face of overwhelming despair. And in his unwavering loyalty to Prince Rama, he embodies the virtues of devotion and sacrifice, inspiring all who witness his deeds to strive for greatness and live a life of virtue and integrity.

As the epic journey of the Ramayana draws to a close, Hanuman Ji's legacy of wisdom and service lives on, inspiring countless generations with his timeless teachings and profound example. For in the heart of every devotee beats the spirit of Hanuman Ji—a spirit that knows no fear, no doubt, and no defeat, but only the boundless love and devotion for his beloved lord.

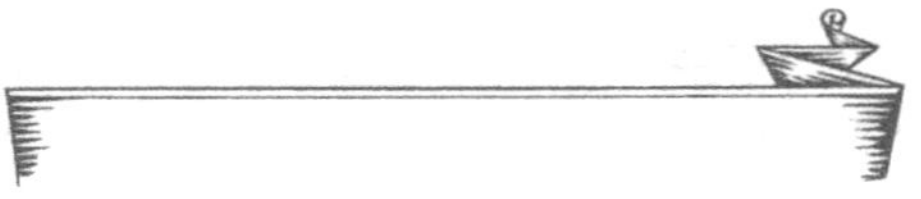

The Knowledge of Devotion

In the epic journey of the Ramayana, Hanuman Ji embodies the profound knowledge that comes from unwavering devotion and surrender to a higher power. Through his unwavering commitment to serving his beloved lord Prince Rama, Hanuman Ji becomes a living testament to the transformative power of devotion, inspiring all who witness his deeds to walk the path of righteousness and virtue.

At the heart of Hanuman Ji's journey lies his deep and abiding love for Prince Rama, a love that transcends mortal understanding and binds him to his beloved lord with bonds of unwavering loyalty and devotion. From the moment he first sets eyes on Prince Rama, Hanuman Ji recognizes him as his divine master and dedicates himself wholeheartedly to serving him in every way possible.

But it is not just blind devotion that drives Hanuman Ji—it is also the profound knowledge that comes from a life lived in service to a higher cause. As he traverses the length and breadth of the Indian subcontinent in search of Sita, he draws upon the teachings of the sage Narada and the wisdom of his own experiences, using them to guide his actions and illuminate the path of righteousness for all who follow in his footsteps.

One of the most profound lessons that Hanuman Ji imparts through his devotion is the importance of surrendering one's own will to the will of a higher power. Despite the countless obstacles and challenges that he faces along his journey, he never wavers in his commitment to serving his beloved lord, trusting implicitly in Prince Rama's wisdom and guidance to lead him on the right path.

In his interactions with Sita, Hanuman Ji demonstrates the true meaning of unconditional love and devotion, offering her solace and comfort in her darkest hour and never faltering in his resolve to reunite her with Prince Rama. And in his unwavering loyalty to Prince Rama, he becomes a beacon of hope and inspiration for all who seek to walk the path of righteousness and virtue.

As the epic journey of the Ramayana draws to a close, Hanuman Ji's legacy of devotion lives on, inspiring countless generations with his timeless example of unwavering love and surrender to a higher power. For in the heart of every devotee beats the spirit of Hanuman Ji—a spirit that knows no fear, no doubt, and no defeat, but only the boundless love and devotion for his beloved lord.

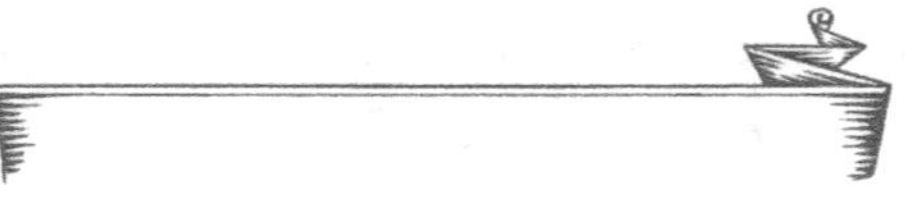

The Insight of Divine Connection

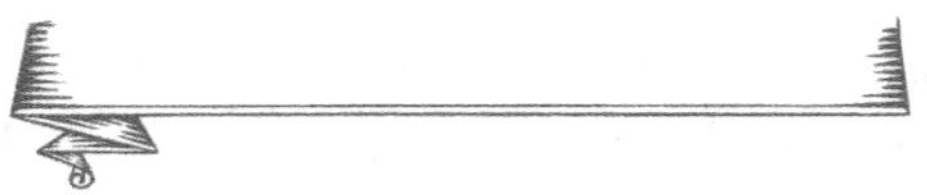

In the grand tapestry of the Ramayana, Hanuman Ji embodies the profound insight that comes from forging a deep and intimate connection with the divine. Through his unwavering devotion and surrender to his beloved lord Prince Rama, Hanuman Ji transcends the limitations of mortal understanding, attaining a level of insight and wisdom that illuminates the path of righteousness for all who seek to follow in his footsteps.

From the moment he first sets eyes on Prince Rama, Hanuman Ji recognizes him as his divine master and dedicates himself wholeheartedly to serving him in every way possible. It is this profound connection with the divine that serves as the guiding force behind all of Hanuman Ji's actions, allowing him to navigate the trials and tribulations of his heroic journey with unwavering faith and clarity of purpose.

But it is not just blind faith that drives Hanuman Ji—it is also the deep and intimate connection that he shares with his beloved lord. Through his unwavering devotion and surrender to Prince Rama's will, Hanuman Ji becomes a vessel for divine grace, allowing the wisdom and power of his beloved lord to flow through him and guide his every action.

As he traverses the length and breadth of the Indian subcontinent in search of Sita, Hanuman Ji draws upon this divine connection to overcome the countless obstacles and challenges that lie in his path. With each step he takes and each trial he faces, he becomes more deeply attuned to the divine presence that surrounds him, allowing him to see beyond the surface of things and perceive the underlying truth that lies at the heart of all creation.

In his interactions with Sita, Hanuman Ji demonstrates the profound insight that comes from surrendering one's own will to the will of a higher power. Despite the darkness that surrounds her and the despair that threatens to consume her, he remains steadfast in his commitment to serving his beloved lord, trusting implicitly in Prince Rama's wisdom and guidance to lead him on the right path.

As the epic journey of the Ramayana draws to a close, Hanuman Ji's legacy of divine connection lives on, inspiring countless generations with his timeless example of unwavering faith and surrender to a higher power. For in the heart of every devotee beats the spirit of Hanuman Ji—a spirit that knows no fear, no doubt, and no defeat, but only the boundless love and devotion for his beloved lord.

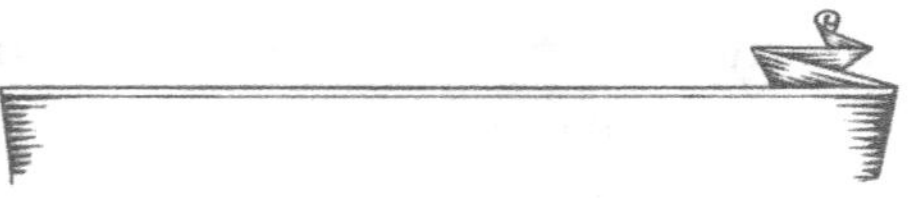

The Eternal Flame of Inspiration

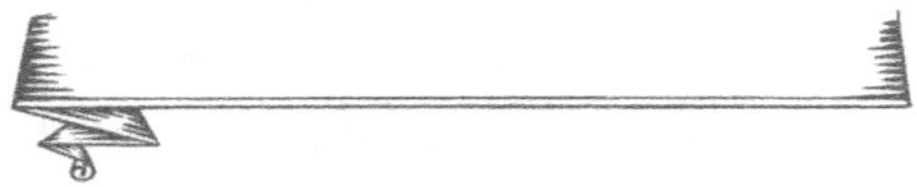

As the epic tale of the Ramayana draws to a close, Hanuman Ji's legacy burns brightly as an eternal flame of inspiration, illuminating the hearts and minds of all who seek to follow in his footsteps. Through his unwavering devotion, boundless courage, and profound wisdom, Hanuman Ji becomes a timeless symbol of righteousness and virtue, inspiring countless generations to strive for greatness and live a life of unwavering devotion to a higher cause.

Hanuman Ji's journey is not just a story of heroic deeds and epic battles—it is also a profound spiritual odyssey that resonates with the deepest longings of the human soul. From his humble beginnings as a divine messenger to his triumphant victory over the forces of evil, Hanuman Ji's quest for self-discovery and enlightenment serves as a powerful reminder of the transformative power of devotion and surrender to a higher power.

But perhaps the truest legacy of Hanuman Ji lies not in the tales of his heroic exploits, but in the timeless wisdom that he imparts to all who seek his guidance. Through his unwavering commitment to serving his beloved lord Prince Rama, Hanuman Ji demonstrates the importance of surrendering one's own will to the will of a higher power, trusting implicitly in divine guidance to lead us on the right path.

In his interactions with Sita, Hanuman Ji embodies the virtues of compassion, selflessness, and unconditional love, offering her solace and comfort in her darkest hour and never wavering in his resolve to reunite her with Prince Rama. And in his unwavering loyalty to his beloved lord, he becomes a beacon of hope and inspiration for all who seek to walk the path of righteousness and virtue.

As we reflect on the legacy of Hanuman Ji, let us remember the timeless wisdom that he imparts to all who seek his guidance, inspiring us to strive for greatness and live a life of unwavering devotion to a higher cause. For in the heart of every devotee beats the spirit of Hanuman Ji—a spirit that knows no fear, no doubt, and no defeat, but only the boundless love and devotion for his beloved lord.

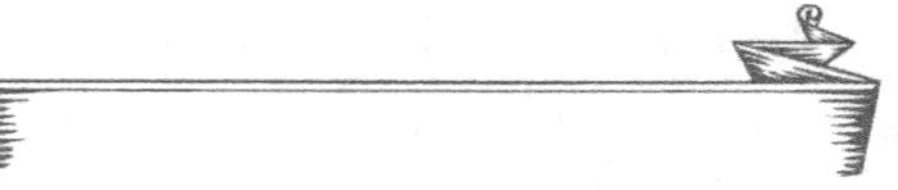

The Eternal Flame of Devotion: Hanuman Ji's Enduring Influence

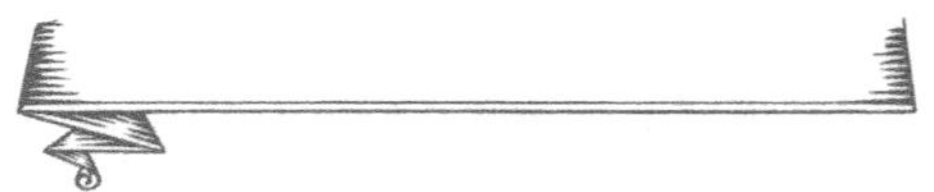

In the vast tapestry of Hindu mythology, few figures shine as brightly as Hanuman Ji, whose unwavering devotion and selfless service have left an indelible mark on the hearts and minds of millions around the world. As we delve deeper into the legacy of Hanuman Ji, we uncover a wealth of stories, teachings, and timeless wisdom that continue to inspire and uplift humanity to this day.

At the heart of Hanuman Ji's story lies his deep and abiding love for his beloved lord Prince Rama, a love that transcends mortal understanding and binds him to his master with bonds of unwavering loyalty and devotion. From the moment he first sets eyes on Prince Rama, Hanuman Ji recognizes him as his divine master and dedicates himself wholeheartedly to serving him in every way possible.

But Hanuman Ji's devotion is not blind—it is rooted in a profound understanding of the divine and a deep connection to the cosmic forces that govern the universe. Through his unwavering faith and surrender to Prince Rama's will, Hanuman Ji becomes a vessel for divine grace, allowing the wisdom and power of his beloved lord to flow through him and guide his every action.

As Hanuman Ji embarks on his epic journey to locate Sita, who has been abducted by the demon king Ravana, he encounters countless obstacles and challenges that test his resolve and faith. But with each trial he faces, he emerges stronger and more steadfast in his commitment to serving his beloved lord, his unwavering devotion serving as a guiding light in the darkness.

Throughout his journey, Hanuman Ji's unwavering devotion and selfless service inspire all who encounter him, from the humblest peasant to the mightiest warrior. His acts of courage, compassion, and sacrifice serve as a beacon of hope and inspiration for generations to come, reminding us of the enduring power of love, loyalty, and faith in the face of adversity.

As we reflect on the legacy of Hanuman Ji, let us remember the timeless lessons that he imparts to us—that true greatness lies not in the power we wield or the accolades we receive, but in the love, loyalty, and faith that we embody in our hearts. For in the heart of every devotee beats the spirit of Hanuman Ji—a spirit that knows no fear, no doubt, and no defeat, but only the boundless love and devotion for his beloved lord.

In carrying forth the flame of devotion that Hanuman Ji has ignited within us, let us strive to live our lives with the same unwavering faith and commitment that he demonstrated throughout his epic journey. For in doing so, we honor not only the legacy of Hanuman Ji, but the timeless principles of righteousness and virtue that he embodies.

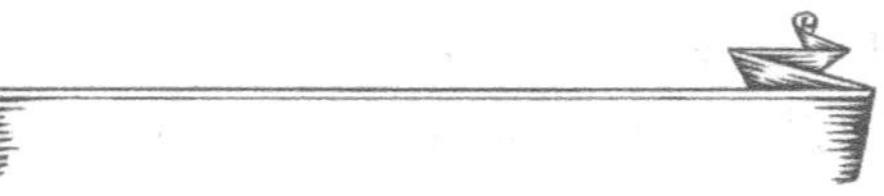

Poem:- The Eternal Devotion of Hanuman Ji

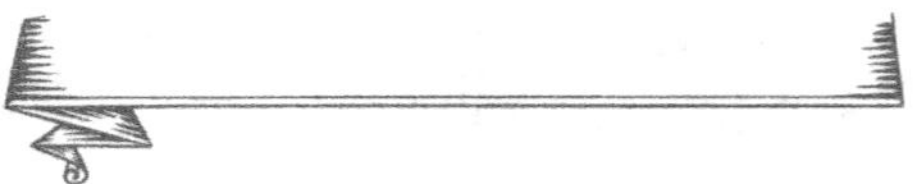

In lands where legends dance on ancient breeze,
Where gods and mortals meet 'neath ancient trees,
There dwells a figure, mighty and divine,
Whose name in every heart does brightly shine.
Hanuman, son of wind and sky above,
Embodiment of courage, strength, and love,
With heart aflame and soul forever free,
He serves his lord with boundless loyalty.
In Lanka's depths, where shadows darkly lay,
He sought the captive princess, gone astray,
Through trials dire and dangers all around,
He leapt with faith, his purpose ever found.
With every bound, he crossed the ocean wide,
His love for Rama burning deep inside,
Through forests dense and mountains towering high,
He searched until he found her, by and by.
In Sita's sorrow, he found his own pain,
Yet comforted her, though all seemed in vain,
With gentle words and tender, loving care,
He offered hope amidst the deep despair.
His loyalty unwavering and true,

He fought for Rama, battles fierce and new,
With every blow, his valor did resound,
His name a beacon, by all warriors found.
But more than strength and courage, he did show,
A wisdom deep that all should come to know,
For in his heart, he held the key to grace,
And found in service, freedom's sweet embrace.
So let us heed the lesson of his tale,
And in our hearts, let Hanuman prevail,
For in his devotion, we find the light,
That guides us through the darkest, stormy night.

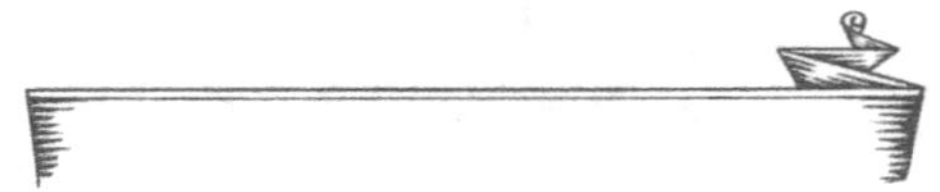

Hanuman Ji's Loyalty and Service

A Divine Promise

In the hallowed halls of the celestial realm, amidst the whispers of wind and the shimmering light of the stars, Hanuman Ji's story begins with a divine promise—one that would bind him to his beloved lord Prince Rama for eternity.

Born of the wind god Vayu and the celestial nymph Anjana, Hanuman Ji was destined for greatness from the moment of his birth. As he grew, his strength and courage surpassed that of all others, earning him the admiration of both gods and mortals alike.

But it was not just physical prowess that set Hanuman Ji apart—it was also his unwavering loyalty and devotion to his beloved lord Prince Rama. From the moment he first laid eyes on Prince Rama, Hanuman Ji recognized him as his divine master and dedicated himself wholeheartedly to serving him in every way possible.

It was this divine promise that would shape the course of Hanuman Ji's life, guiding him through the trials and tribulations that lay ahead and inspiring him to perform acts of unparalleled heroism and sacrifice.

As the epic tale of the Ramayana unfolds, we witness Hanuman Ji's unwavering loyalty in action, as he embarks on a perilous journey to locate Sita, who has been abducted by the demon king Ravana. Despite the countless dangers that lie in his path, Hanuman Ji remains steadfast in his commitment to serving his beloved lord, his heart aflame with the fire of righteousness.

With each bound he takes, he draws closer to his goal, his unwavering faith guiding him through the darkness that surrounds him. And when he finally locates Sita amidst the ruins of the fortress in Lanka, his heart swells with love and devotion, knowing that he has fulfilled his divine promise to his beloved lord.

But the true test of Hanuman Ji's loyalty is yet to come, as he must now return to Prince Rama and deliver the news of Sita's whereabouts. With a heavy heart and a sense of duty that knows no bounds, Hanuman Ji sets forth on his journey back to his beloved lord, his unwavering loyalty shining brightly in the face of adversity.

As we reflect on the unwavering loyalty of Hanuman Ji, let us remember the timeless lessons that he imparts to us—that true greatness lies not in the power we wield or the accolades we receive, but in the love, loyalty, and devotion that we embody in our hearts. For in the heart of every devotee beats the spirit of Hanuman Ji—a spirit that knows no fear, no doubt, and no defeat, but only the boundless love and devotion for his beloved lord.

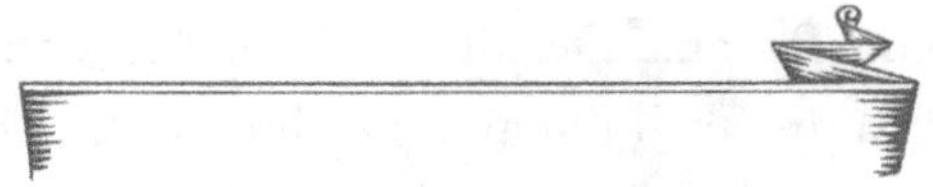

The Trials of Loyalty: A Journey of Sacrifice

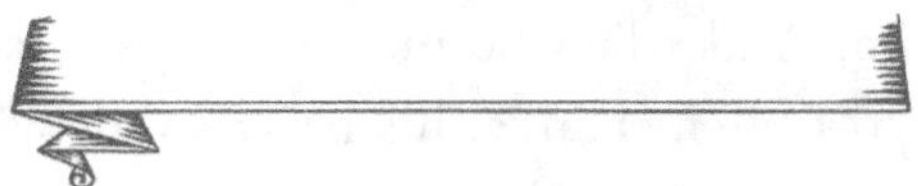

As Hanuman Ji's journey unfolds, his unwavering loyalty to Prince Rama is put to the test in ways he could never have imagined. With each trial he faces, his commitment to serving his beloved lord is strengthened, his resolve deepening with every obstacle overcome.

Upon his return from Lanka, Hanuman Ji finds himself faced with the daunting task of delivering the news of Sita's whereabouts to Prince Rama. But even as he approaches his beloved lord, doubts begin to gnaw at his heart, whispering of the dangers that lie ahead and the uncertainty of the future.

Yet, despite the darkness that surrounds him, Hanuman Ji remains steadfast in his commitment to serving his beloved lord, his unwavering loyalty shining brightly in the face of adversity. With a heavy heart and a sense of duty that knows no bounds, he sets forth on his journey back to Prince Rama, his every step a testament to his undying devotion.

But the road ahead is fraught with peril, as Hanuman Ji soon discovers. Along the way, he encounters foes both old and new, each seeking to thwart his mission and prevent him from delivering the news to Prince Rama. Yet, with each challenge he faces, Hanuman Ji's resolve only grows stronger, his determination to serve his beloved lord unwavering in the face of adversity.

As he traverses forests dense and mountains towering high, Hanuman Ji draws upon his inner strength and the teachings of his beloved lord to overcome every obstacle that lies in his path. With each victory he achieves, his faith in Prince Rama's wisdom and guidance is reaffirmed, his loyalty to his beloved lord shining brightly through the darkness that surrounds him.

And when he finally reaches the side of his beloved lord, weary and battle-worn yet triumphant, Hanuman Ji's heart swells with love and devotion, knowing that he has fulfilled his divine promise once more. For in the heart of every devotee beats the spirit of Hanuman Ji—a spirit that knows no fear, no doubt, and no defeat, but only the boundless love and devotion for his beloved lord.

The Depths of Devotion: A Sacrifice of Self

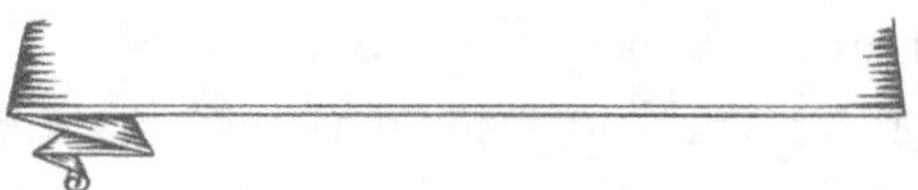

As Hanuman Ji's journey continues, his unwavering loyalty to Prince Rama is tested in ways that demand the ultimate sacrifice—the sacrifice of self. For true loyalty knows no bounds, and Hanuman Ji's devotion to his beloved lord transcends even the limitations of his own identity.

In his quest to serve Prince Rama, Hanuman Ji must confront the very essence of his being, surrendering his ego and sense of self to the greater purpose that he serves. This sacrifice is not one of physical prowess or heroic deeds, but of the deepest recesses of his soul—the very core of his being.

As he stands before Prince Rama, humbled and awed by the presence of his beloved lord, Hanuman Ji realizes that his journey is not just about serving his master, but about surrendering himself completely to the divine will that guides him. In this moment of realization, he lets go of all attachment to his own desires and ambitions, offering himself up as a vessel for divine grace and guidance.

With each act of service and sacrifice, Hanuman Ji's sense of self diminishes, replaced by an overwhelming sense of oneness with his beloved lord. He becomes not just a servant, but a reflection of Prince Rama's own divine nature, his every thought and action guided by the love and devotion that binds him to his master.

But even as he surrenders himself completely to the will of his beloved lord, Hanuman Ji does not lose himself in the process. Instead, he finds a deeper sense of purpose and fulfillment than he ever thought possible, his every action infused with the boundless love and devotion that flows from his heart.

In this sacrifice of self, Hanuman Ji discovers the true meaning of loyalty—the willingness to give oneself completely to a higher cause, regardless of the cost. For in the end, it is not the deeds we perform or the accolades we receive that define us, but the love, loyalty, and devotion that we embody in our hearts.

As we reflect on the depths of devotion displayed by Hanuman Ji, let us remember the timeless lessons that he imparts to us—that true greatness lies not in the power we wield or the recognition we receive, but in the love, loyalty, and devotion that we offer up to a higher cause. For in the heart of every devotee beats the spirit of Hanuman Ji—a spirit that knows no fear, no doubt, and no defeat, but only the boundless love and devotion for his beloved lord.

The Essence of Service: An Offering of Devotion

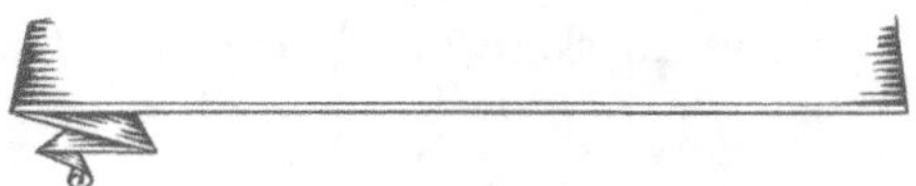

As Hanuman Ji's journey of loyalty and service continues, he embodies the essence of selfless devotion, offering himself up completely to the service of his beloved lord Prince Rama. In this act of surrender, he becomes a living testament to the transformative power of service, inspiring all who witness his deeds to strive for greatness and live a life of unwavering dedication to a higher cause.

With each passing day, Hanuman Ji's commitment to serving Prince Rama deepens, his every thought and action guided by the love and devotion that burns brightly within his heart. No task is too great, no sacrifice too small, as he dedicates himself wholeheartedly to fulfilling his divine promise to his beloved lord.

But it is not just the magnitude of his deeds that sets Hanuman Ji apart—it is also the purity of his intentions and the depth of his love for his master. Every act of service is imbued with a sense of reverence and devotion, as he seeks not just to fulfill his duty, but to express his love and gratitude to his beloved lord.

In his interactions with Prince Rama, Hanuman Ji demonstrates the true essence of service, offering himself up completely to the will of his master and finding fulfillment in the act of giving. Whether he is acting as a messenger, a warrior, or a friend, his every action is guided by the desire to serve his beloved lord to the best of his abilities.

And it is this selfless devotion that earns Hanuman Ji the highest praise and honor from his beloved lord, as Prince Rama recognizes the depth of his love and devotion and bestows upon him his eternal gratitude and friendship.

As we reflect on the essence of service embodied by Hanuman Ji, let us remember the timeless lessons that he imparts to us—that true greatness lies not in the recognition we receive or the rewards we attain, but in the love, loyalty, and devotion that we offer up to a higher cause. For in the heart of every devotee beats the spirit of Hanuman Ji—a spirit that knows no fear, no doubt, and no defeat, but only the boundless love and devotion for his beloved lord.

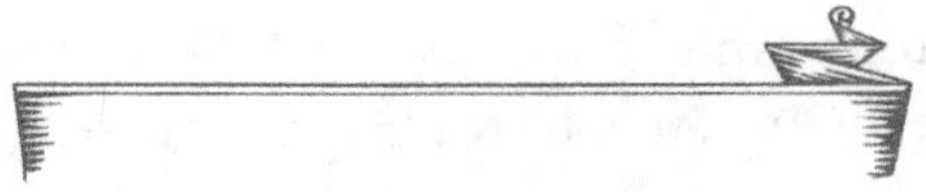

The Sacred Vow: A Bond Eternal

In the grand tapestry of the Ramayana, Hanuman Ji's unwavering loyalty to Prince Rama reaches its zenith, as he makes a sacred vow that binds him to his beloved lord for eternity. In this moment of solemn promise, Hanuman Ji transcends the limitations of mortal understanding, forging a bond of love and devotion that will endure throughout the ages.

As Hanuman Ji stands before his beloved lord, his heart overflowing with love and gratitude, he offers up a vow that echoes through the heavens, a testament to the depth of his devotion and the strength of his commitment. With each word he speaks, his bond with Prince Rama grows stronger, his every thought and action guided by the love and loyalty that binds him to his master.

But it is not just the words of his vow that define Hanuman Ji's commitment—it is also the sincerity of his intentions and the purity of his heart. In making this sacred promise, he offers up his very soul to Prince Rama, pledging himself to a life of unwavering service and devotion.

As the echoes of his vow fade into the distance, Hanuman Ji stands before his beloved lord, his heart filled with a sense of peace and contentment. For in that moment, he knows that he has given himself completely to the service of his master, his every thought and action guided by the love and devotion that burns brightly within his heart.

And so, as the epic journey of the Ramayana draws to a close, Hanuman Ji's sacred vow stands as a testament to the enduring power of love and devotion. For in the heart of every devotee beats the spirit of Hanuman Ji—a spirit that knows no fear, no doubt, and no defeat, but only the boundless love and devotion for his beloved lord.

The Eternal Bond of Hanuman Ji's Devotion: A Legacy of Love

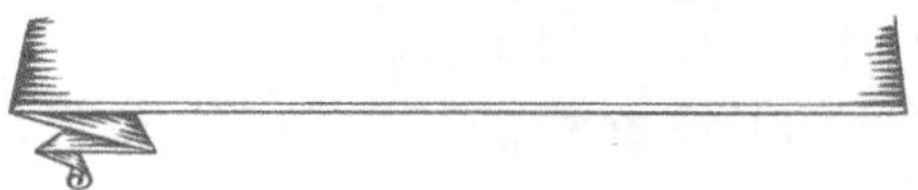

In the annals of time, amidst the pages of ancient scriptures and the whispers of devotees' prayers, the legacy of Hanuman Ji's unwavering devotion continues to shine brightly, illuminating the hearts and minds of all who seek solace in the embrace of divine love.

As the embodiment of selfless service and undying loyalty, Hanuman Ji's sacred vow to Prince Rama transcends the boundaries of mortal understanding, weaving a tapestry of love and devotion that stretches across the ages. His commitment to his beloved lord serves as a timeless example of the boundless potential that lies within the human heart, inspiring generations to come with its profound depth and unwavering sincerity.

But beyond the mere words of his vow lies the essence of Hanuman Ji's devotion—a love so pure, so unconditional, that it knows no bounds. In every action, every thought, every beat of his heart, he is guided by the love and devotion that flows freely from the depths of his soul, binding him eternally to his beloved lord.

In his interactions with Prince Rama, Hanuman Ji exemplifies the true meaning of love and devotion, offering himself up completely to the service of his master with a joy and humility that knows no equal. Whether he is acting as a messenger, a warrior, or a friend, his every deed is infused with the sacred essence of love, a testament to the depth of his devotion and the purity of his heart.

And it is this eternal bond of love and devotion that continues to inspire and uplift humanity to this day, serving as a guiding light for all who seek refuge in the embrace of divine love. For in the heart of every devotee beats the spirit of Hanuman Ji—a spirit that knows no fear, no doubt, and no defeat, but only the boundless love and devotion for his beloved lord.

As we reflect on the legacy of Hanuman Ji, let us remember the timeless lessons that he imparts to us—that true greatness lies not in the recognition we receive or the rewards we attain, but in the love, loyalty, and devotion that we offer up to a higher cause. For in the heart of every devotee beats the spirit of Hanuman Ji—a spirit that knows no fear, no doubt, and no defeat, but only the boundless love and devotion for his beloved lord.

Poem: Hanuman Ji: The Embodiment of Devotion

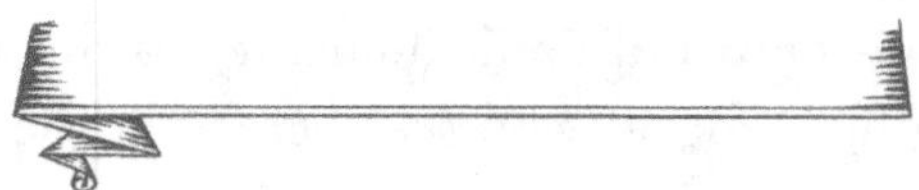

In the realm of ancient lore, where gods and mortals meet,
There dwells a figure noble, with devotion pure and sweet.
Hanuman Ji, son of wind, with heart as vast as sky,
Embodies love and loyalty that never shall run dry.
With every bound he takes, across the oceans wide,
His love for Rama burns bright, an everlasting guide.
Through forests dense and mountains tall, he journeys without fear,
His devotion unwavering, his purpose ever clear.
In Sita's sorrow, he finds his own heart's pain,
Yet offers her comfort, amidst darkness and disdain.
With gentle words and tender care, he soothes her troubled soul,
His love a beacon in the night, making broken spirits whole.
In battles fierce, on Lanka's shore, he stands with courage bold,
A warrior for righteousness, in service manifold.
With each blow struck and foe vanquished, he honors his dear lord,

His devotion shining brightly, like a flame in the darkened
horde.
But beyond his deeds of valor, his heart remains aglow,
With love and devotion that only true devotees know.
For in the heart of Hanuman Ji, burns a sacred flame,
A love for Prince Rama that forever shall remain.
So let us heed the lessons of this noble devotee,
And strive to live with love and devotion, pure and free.
For in the heart of every soul, may Hanuman Ji reside,
A beacon of devotion, forever by our side.
Jai Shri Ram!

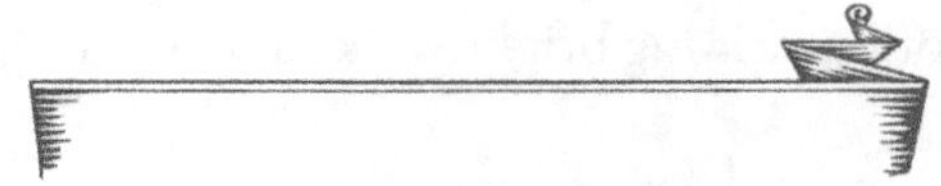

Hanuman Ji's Leadership and Influence

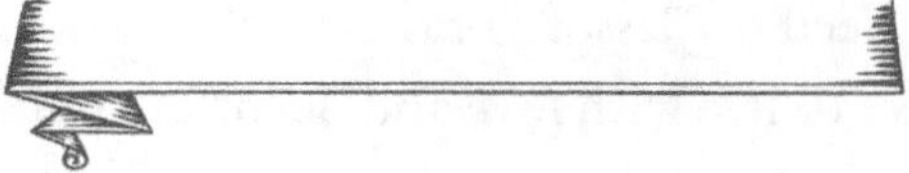

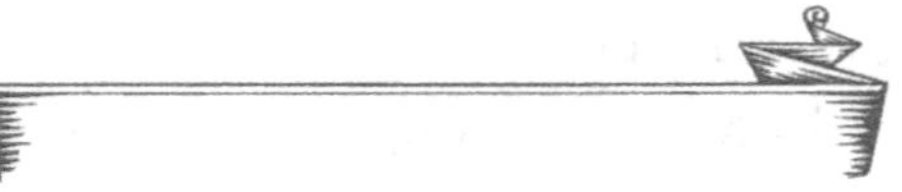

Hanuman Ji: The Leader Amongst Devotees: A Call to Leadership

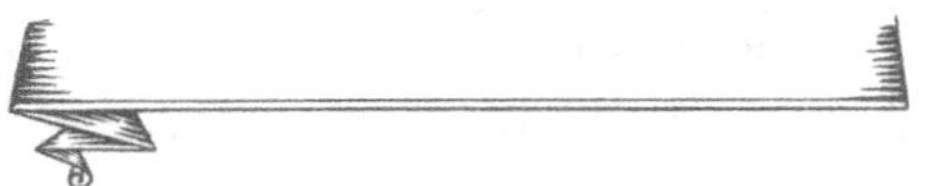

In the grand tapestry of Hindu mythology, amidst the countless stories of gods and heroes, Hanuman Ji emerges as a beacon of leadership, guiding his fellow devotees with wisdom, courage, and compassion. His journey from a humble servant to a revered leader is a testament to the transformative power of devotion and the boundless potential that lies within every soul.

From his earliest encounters with Prince Rama, Hanuman Ji demonstrates the qualities of a true leader—loyalty, selflessness, and unwavering commitment to a higher cause. As he stands by Prince Rama's side through every trial and tribulation, his presence serves as a source of strength and inspiration for all who follow him.

But it is not just Hanuman Ji's actions that define his leadership—it is also his ability to inspire and motivate others to greatness. Whether he is rallying his fellow warriors on the battlefield or offering words of wisdom and guidance to those in need, his leadership shines brightly, illuminating the path forward for all who seek to follow in his footsteps.

As the epic journey of the Ramayana unfolds, Hanuman Ji's leadership is put to the test time and time again, as he navigates the challenges and obstacles that lie in his path. From leading the search for Sita to orchestrating the rescue mission in Lanka, his ability to remain calm, focused, and decisive in the face of adversity serves as a shining example of true leadership.

But perhaps the truest measure of Hanuman Ji's leadership lies not in the battles he wins or the enemies he defeats, but in the hearts and minds of those who follow him. For in the end, it is not the title or position that makes a leader, but the ability to inspire, empower, and uplift those around them.

As we reflect on the leadership of Hanuman Ji, let us remember the timeless lessons that he imparts to us—that true greatness lies not in the power we wield or the recognition we receive, but in the love, loyalty, and devotion that we offer up to a higher cause. For in the heart of every devotee beats the spirit of Hanuman Ji—a spirit that knows no fear, no doubt, and no defeat, but only the boundless love and devotion for his beloved lord.

The Wisdom of Leadership: Guidance Through Knowledge

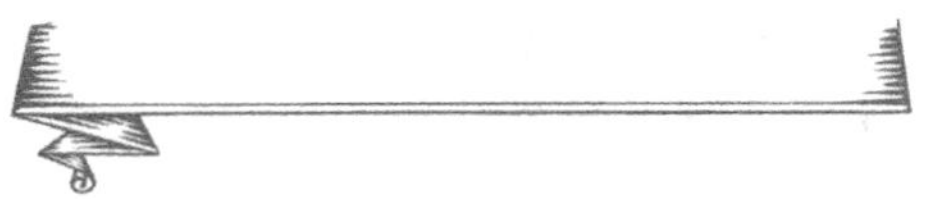

As Hanuman Ji's leadership journey continues, he exemplifies the profound wisdom and insight that are essential qualities of a true leader. His ability to navigate complex situations with clarity and understanding serves as a guiding light for his fellow devotees, inspiring them to rise above challenges and embrace their highest potential.

Throughout his interactions with Prince Rama and his comrades, Hanuman Ji demonstrates a deep understanding of the intricacies of human nature and the complexities of the world around him. Whether he is offering counsel to those in need or making difficult decisions in times of crisis, his wisdom shines brightly, illuminating the path forward with clarity and grace.

But it is not just Hanuman Ji's knowledge of the external world that sets him apart—it is also his deep inner wisdom, cultivated through years of devotion and spiritual practice. In moments of solitude and reflection, he taps into the infinite wellspring of divine wisdom that resides within his heart, drawing upon its boundless depths to guide his actions and decisions.

As he leads his fellow devotees on their journey of righteousness, Hanuman Ji imparts his wisdom with humility and compassion, recognizing that true leadership is not about exerting power or control, but about empowering others to realize their own potential. Whether he is teaching them the importance of righteousness, the value of humility, or the power of devotion, his words resonate deeply, inspiring all who hear them to strive for greatness.

And it is this profound wisdom and insight that earns Hanuman Ji the respect and admiration of all who know him, as they recognize in him a leader who leads not with force, but with wisdom, compassion, and love. For in the heart of every devotee beats the spirit of Hanuman Ji—a spirit that knows no fear, no doubt, and no defeat, but only the boundless love and devotion for his beloved lord.

As we reflect on the wisdom of Hanuman Ji's leadership, let us remember the timeless lessons that he imparts to us—that true greatness lies not in the knowledge we accumulate or the titles we hold, but in the wisdom, humility, and compassion that we embody in our hearts. For in the heart of every devotee beats the spirit of Hanuman Ji—a spirit that guides us ever onward on the path of righteousness and devotion.

Empowering Others: Inspiring Action

Hanuman Ji's leadership journey is not just about his own actions and decisions, but also about empowering others to step into their own greatness. As a true leader, he recognizes the potential within each individual and strives to uplift and inspire them to achieve their highest aspirations.

With his boundless love and compassion, Hanuman Ji creates a supportive and nurturing environment in which others can thrive and grow. He listens with an open heart, offering guidance and encouragement to those who seek his counsel, and empowering them to overcome their fears and limitations.

Through his words and actions, Hanuman Ji instills confidence and courage in his fellow devotees, reminding them of their inherent strength and resilience. He leads by example, demonstrating the power of determination and perseverance in the face of adversity, and inspiring others to do the same.

But perhaps the most profound way in which Hanuman Ji empowers others is through his unwavering belief in their potential. He sees the best in everyone, even when they cannot see it themselves, and encourages them to step into their greatness with confidence and conviction.

In times of doubt and uncertainty, Hanuman Ji is a beacon of hope and inspiration, reminding his fellow devotees of their divine purpose and calling. He helps them to overcome their fears and insecurities, and empowers them to embrace their destiny with courage and grace.

And it is this empowering leadership style that earns Hanuman Ji the undying loyalty and devotion of all who know him. For in the heart of every devotee beats the spirit of Hanuman Ji—a spirit that inspires them to rise above their limitations and achieve their highest potential.

As we reflect on the empowering leadership of Hanuman Ji, let us remember the timeless lessons that he imparts to us—that true greatness lies not in the power we wield over others, but in our ability to uplift and inspire them to achieve their own greatness. For in the heart of every devotee beats the spirit of Hanuman Ji—a spirit that empowers us to embrace our divine purpose and calling.

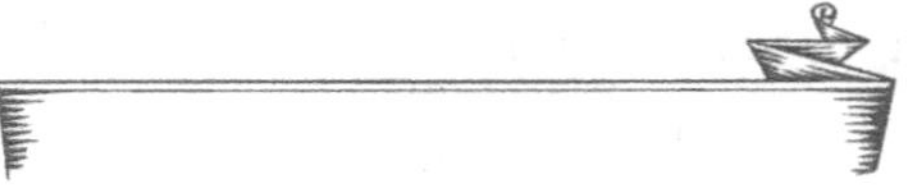

Resilience in Adversity: Leading Through Challenges

Hanuman Ji's leadership journey is not without its challenges and obstacles. Yet, it is in the face of adversity that his true leadership qualities shine brightest. With resilience and determination, he navigates through the darkest of times, guiding his fellow devotees with unwavering strength and courage.

As challenges arise and obstacles loom on the horizon, Hanuman Ji remains steadfast in his commitment to his divine mission. He leads by example, demonstrating to his fellow devotees the importance of resilience and perseverance in the face of adversity.

In times of crisis, Hanuman Ji remains calm and composed, inspiring confidence and courage in those around him. He faces each challenge with unwavering determination, refusing to be swayed by doubt or fear, and empowering others to do the same.

But perhaps the true measure of Hanuman Ji's leadership lies not in his ability to avoid challenges, but in his capacity to transform them into opportunities for growth and learning. He approaches each obstacle as a chance to strengthen his resolve and deepen his connection to his divine purpose.

Through his actions and words, Hanuman Ji instills hope and optimism in his fellow devotees, reminding them that no challenge is insurmountable when faced with courage and determination. He encourages them to embrace adversity as a catalyst for growth, and to emerge stronger and more resilient than ever before.

And it is this unwavering resilience in the face of adversity that earns Hanuman Ji the respect and admiration of all who know him. For in the heart of every devotee beats the spirit of Hanuman Ji—a spirit that knows no defeat, but only the boundless strength and courage to overcome any obstacle.

As we reflect on the resilience of Hanuman Ji's leadership, let us remember the timeless lessons that he imparts to us—that true greatness lies not in the absence of challenges, but in our ability to face them with courage and determination. For in the heart of every devotee beats the spirit of Hanuman Ji—a spirit that inspires us to rise above adversity and achieve our highest aspirations.

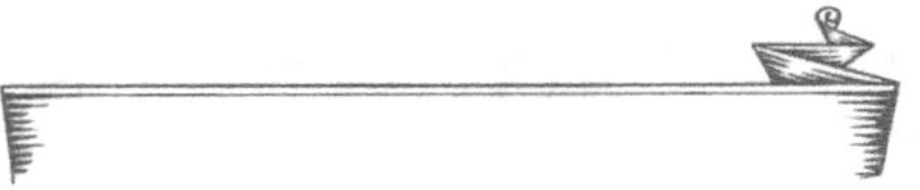

Compassionate Leadership: Leading with Heart

Hanuman Ji's leadership is defined not only by his strength and courage, but also by his boundless compassion and empathy for all beings. As a leader, he leads with his heart, guiding his fellow devotees with kindness, understanding, and love.

In every interaction, Hanuman Ji demonstrates deep empathy and compassion for the struggles and challenges faced by those around him. He listens with an open heart, offering support and encouragement to those in need, and providing solace and comfort to those who are suffering.

With his gentle words and compassionate presence, Hanuman Ji creates a safe and nurturing environment in which others can express themselves freely and openly. He fosters a sense of belonging and community among his fellow devotees, reminding them that they are never alone in their struggles.

But perhaps the most profound way in which Hanuman Ji demonstrates his compassion is through his selfless service to others. He goes out of his way to help those in need, offering assistance and guidance without expecting anything in return. His acts of kindness and generosity inspire others to follow his example, creating a ripple effect of compassion and love that spreads far and wide.

In times of sorrow and despair, Hanuman Ji is a source of hope and healing for his fellow devotees. He offers words of wisdom and comfort, reminding them of the eternal love and support that surrounds them. He leads by example, showing others that true strength lies not in power or dominance, but in the ability to empathize and connect with others on a deep and meaningful level.

And it is this compassionate leadership style that earns Hanuman Ji the undying loyalty and devotion of all who know him. For in the heart of every devotee beats the spirit of Hanuman Ji—a spirit that embodies the true essence of love, compassion, and kindness.

As we reflect on the compassionate leadership of Hanuman Ji, let us remember the timeless lessons that he imparts to us—that true greatness lies not in power or authority, but in the ability to lead with love, compassion, and empathy. For in the heart of every devotee beats the spirit of Hanuman Ji—a spirit that inspires us to lead with kindness and grace in all that we do.

Legacy of Leadership: Inspiring Future Generations

As Hanuman Ji's leadership journey reaches its culmination, his legacy endures as a timeless beacon of inspiration for future generations. Through his exemplary leadership, he leaves behind a profound impact on the hearts and minds of all who have been touched by his wisdom, courage, and compassion.

Hanuman Ji's leadership is not bound by time or space—it transcends the ages, resonating with people from all walks of life and inspiring them to embrace their own leadership potential. His teachings serve as a guiding light for leaders of today and tomorrow, reminding them of the importance of integrity, humility, and service in their roles.

Through stories and legends passed down through the ages, Hanuman Ji's leadership continues to inspire and uplift humanity, offering hope and guidance in times of uncertainty and doubt. His unwavering commitment to righteousness and devotion serves as a reminder that true leadership is rooted in love, compassion, and selflessness.

But perhaps the greatest testament to Hanuman Ji's leadership is the impact he has on the hearts and minds of those who follow him. His devotees are inspired to embody his teachings in their own lives, striving to lead with integrity, courage, and compassion in all that they do.

As we reflect on the legacy of Hanuman Ji's leadership, let us remember the timeless lessons that he imparts to us—that true greatness lies not in the recognition we receive or the power we wield, but in the love, compassion, and service that we offer to others. For in the heart of every devotee beats the spirit of Hanuman Ji—a spirit that inspires us to lead with courage, humility, and love.

Poem:

In the heart of devotion's flame,
Resides the one who bears no name.
With boundless strength and spirit pure,
Hanuman Ji, forever endure.
Across the skies, his mighty leap,
A testament to love so deep.
In service to his lord's command,
He soars across the timeless land.
With heart aflame and eyes aglow,
Through darkest night and fiercest foe.
His courage shines, a guiding light,
In every trial, in every fight.
In Sita's sorrow, he finds his own,
A love that's true, forever shown.
With gentle words and caring hand,
He brings solace to a troubled land.
In battles fierce, on Lanka's shore,
He stands with courage evermore.
A warrior brave, in righteous fight,
Dispelling darkness with his might.
But beyond his strength and valor bold,
Lies a heart of purest gold.

In every deed, in every part,
Resides the love that fills his heart.
So let us raise our voices high,
In praise of him who touches sky.
For in the heart of every devotee,
Resides the spirit of Hanuman Ji.
Jai Shri Ram!

Hanuman Ji's Symbolism and Significance

Hanuman Ji: The Symbol of Devotion, Origin and Symbolism

Hanuman Ji, the beloved devotee of Lord Rama, embodies the essence of devotion and selflessness in Hindu mythology. His symbolism and significance are deeply rooted in the ancient scriptures and traditions, reflecting profound spiritual truths that resonate with devotees across generations.

Born to Anjana and Kesari, Hanuman Ji is said to be the son of the wind god, Vayu. His birth is shrouded in legend, with tales of divine intervention and celestial blessings. According to mythology, he was born with great strength and intelligence, destined to play a pivotal role in the epic tale of the Ramayana.

As a symbol, Hanuman Ji represents unwavering devotion and loyalty to the divine. His boundless love for Lord Rama and selfless service to him are revered as the highest ideals of bhakti (devotion) in Hinduism. He is often depicted with folded hands, bowing in reverence to his beloved lord, symbolizing the surrender of the ego and the recognition of the divine presence within all beings.

Hanuman Ji's physical attributes also hold symbolic significance. His monkey form represents humility and simplicity, reminding devotees to let go of pride and ego in their spiritual journey. His large, powerful frame symbolizes strength and courage, inspiring devotees to overcome obstacles and face challenges with resilience and determination.

Furthermore, Hanuman Ji's role as a messenger and bridge-builder in the Ramayana carries deeper symbolic meaning. As a messenger, he represents the divine intermediary between the mortal and the divine, carrying messages of hope and guidance from the heavens to the earth. As a bridge-builder, he symbolizes the connection between the material and the spiritual realms, bridging the gap between human limitations and divine possibilities.

In Hindu iconography, Hanuman Ji is often depicted holding a mace (gada) and a mountain (Parvat), symbolizing his immense strength and power. His devotion to Lord Rama is symbolized by the tilak (sacred mark) on his forehead, which is said to contain the name of Rama inscribed in his heart.

Overall, Hanuman Ji's symbolism and significance are multifaceted, embodying the highest ideals of devotion, courage, and selflessness in Hindu mythology. His story serves as a timeless reminder of the power of faith and the boundless love that exists between the devotee and the divine.

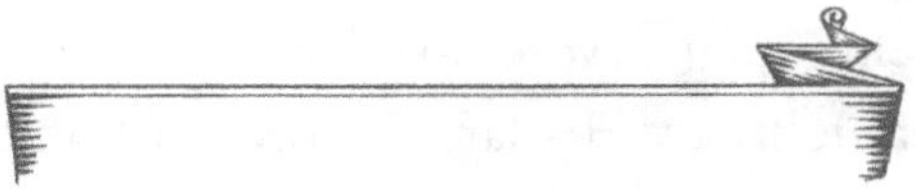

The Embodiment of Bhakti: Devotion in Action

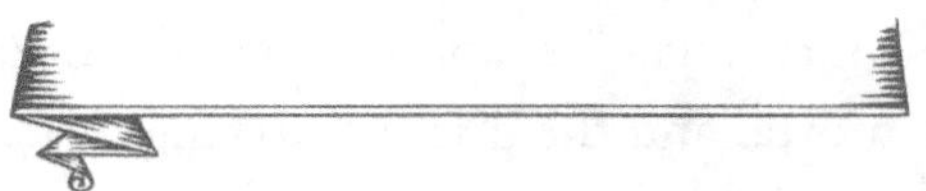

Hanuman Ji's significance as the embodiment of devotion is exemplified through his actions and deeds in the epic tale of the Ramayana. His unwavering love and commitment to Lord Rama serve as a timeless example of bhakti (devotion) in action, inspiring devotees to deepen their own spiritual practice and cultivate a deeper connection with the divine.

From his first encounter with Lord Rama in the forest of Kishkindha, Hanuman Ji's devotion shines brightly, illuminating the path of righteousness for all who witness it. He recognizes Lord Rama as the embodiment of divinity and surrenders himself completely to his service, becoming his most trusted and loyal devotee.

Throughout the Ramayana, Hanuman Ji's devotion is put to the test time and time again, as he faces numerous challenges and obstacles in service to his beloved lord. Whether he is leaping across the ocean to reach Lanka, battling demons in the forest, or rescuing Sita from the clutches of Ravana, his love for Lord Rama remains unwavering, driving him forward with courage and determination.

But perhaps the truest testament to Hanuman Ji's devotion lies in his selfless service to others. Despite his immense power and strength, he never seeks recognition or reward for his actions, but simply acts out of love and devotion for his beloved lord. He sacrifices his own comfort and safety for the sake of others, demonstrating the highest ideals of bhakti in action.

Hanuman Ji's devotion is not limited to his service to Lord Rama alone, but extends to all beings. He sees the divine presence in every living being and treats all with kindness, compassion, and respect. His unconditional love knows no bounds, inspiring devotees to cultivate a similar attitude of love and service towards all of creation.

In essence, Hanuman Ji's life serves as a living testament to the power of devotion to transform lives and transcend limitations. Through his unwavering love and commitment to Lord Rama, he inspires devotees to deepen their own spiritual practice and cultivate a deeper connection with the divine.

As we reflect on the embodiment of devotion that is Hanuman Ji, let us remember the timeless lessons that he imparts to us—that true greatness lies not in power or prestige, but in the depth of our love and devotion to the divine. For in the heart of every devotee beats the spirit of Hanuman Ji—a spirit that inspires us to surrender ourselves completely to the service of the divine.

The Eternal Servant: Loyalty and Service

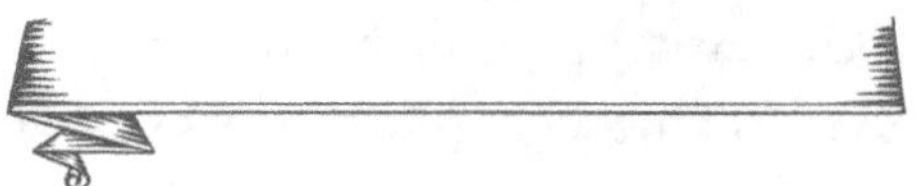

Hanuman Ji's significance as the eternal servant of Lord Rama is deeply rooted in his unwavering loyalty and selfless service. Throughout the epic of the Ramayana, his devotion to his beloved lord knows no bounds, as he tirelessly serves him with love, dedication, and humility.

From the moment Hanuman Ji pledges his allegiance to Lord Rama, he becomes the epitome of loyalty, never wavering in his commitment to his divine master. His loyalty is unwavering, even in the face of seemingly insurmountable challenges and obstacles. He remains steadfast in his devotion, standing by Lord Rama's side through every trial and tribulation.

Hanuman Ji's service to Lord Rama is characterized by humility and selflessness, as he puts aside his own needs and desires in service to his beloved lord. Whether he is acting as a messenger, a warrior, or a friend, his every action is guided by his deep love and devotion for Lord Rama.

But perhaps the truest measure of Hanuman Ji's loyalty and service lies in his willingness to sacrifice everything for the sake of his beloved lord. He risks life and limb countless times in service to Lord Rama, facing death and danger with unwavering courage and determination.

In his selfless devotion, Hanuman Ji embodies the highest ideals of servitude and devotion, inspiring devotees to emulate his example in their own lives. His humility, loyalty, and selflessness serve as a timeless reminder of the power of service to transform lives and uplift humanity.

As we reflect on Hanuman Ji's eternal service to Lord Rama, let us remember the timeless lessons that he imparts to us—that true greatness lies not in power or prestige, but in the depth of our love and devotion to the divine. For in the heart of every devotee beats the spirit of Hanuman Ji—a spirit that inspires us to serve with humility, loyalty, and selflessness in all that we do.

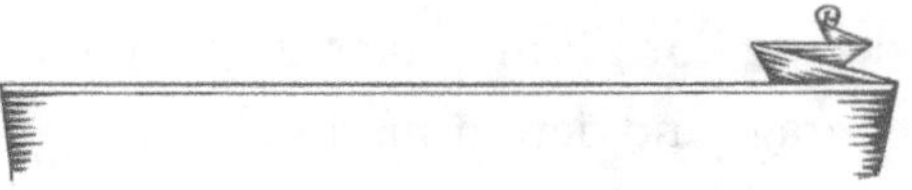

The Embodiment of Strength: Power and Protection

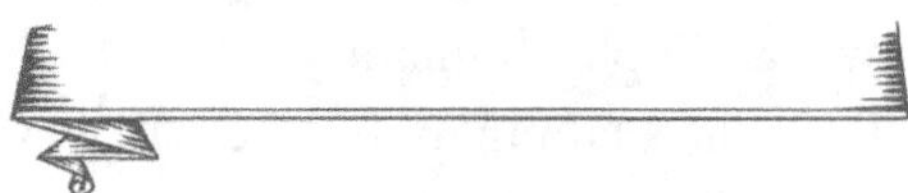

Hanuman Ji's significance as the embodiment of strength is reflected in his unparalleled power and ability to protect those in need. Throughout the epic of the Ramayana, his strength and prowess are showcased in numerous feats of heroism and valor, earning him the admiration and reverence of all who witness his deeds.

From his earliest encounters with Lord Rama, Hanuman Ji's strength is evident, as he demonstrates his ability to leap across vast distances and perform incredible feats of strength and agility. His physical prowess is unmatched, making him a formidable warrior and protector of righteousness.

But Hanuman Ji's strength is not merely physical—it is also spiritual and emotional. His unwavering faith and devotion to Lord Rama give him the inner strength and courage to face any challenge or obstacle that comes his way. He draws upon the power of his devotion to overcome adversity and protect those in need.

Throughout the Ramayana, Hanuman Ji uses his strength to protect and defend the innocent, standing up against injustice and tyranny wherever he finds it. Whether he is battling demons in the forest or rescuing Sita from the clutches of Ravana, his strength is always guided by his sense of righteousness and compassion.

But perhaps the most profound aspect of Hanuman Ji's strength lies in his ability to protect the spiritual well-being of his devotees. Through his teachings and guidance, he offers protection from the forces of ignorance and illusion, leading his followers on the path of righteousness and enlightenment.

In his role as the protector of righteousness, Hanuman Ji embodies the highest ideals of strength and courage, inspiring devotees to cultivate these qualities in their own lives. His example serves as a reminder of the power of faith and devotion to overcome any obstacle and achieve victory over darkness.

As we reflect on Hanuman Ji's embodiment of strength, let us remember the timeless lessons that he imparts to us—that true greatness lies not in physical power alone, but in the strength of character and the depth of devotion to the divine. For in the heart of every devotee beats the spirit of Hanuman Ji—a spirit that inspires us to cultivate strength and courage in all that we do.

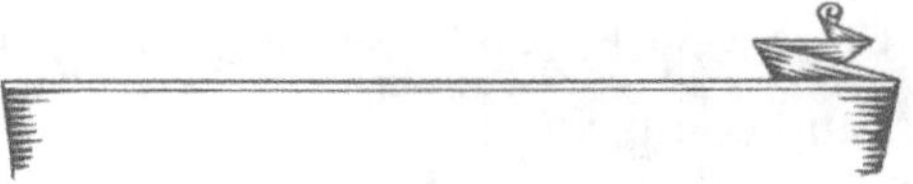

The Messenger of Wisdom: Knowledge and Guidance

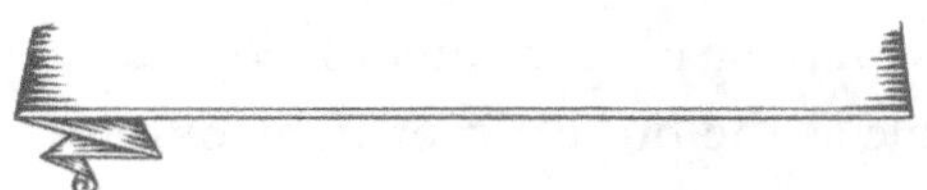

Hanuman Ji's significance as the messenger of wisdom is deeply intertwined with his role as a source of guidance and enlightenment for seekers of truth. Throughout the Ramayana, he imparts valuable teachings and insights that serve as a beacon of light for those on the path of righteousness.

With his vast knowledge and keen intellect, Hanuman Ji offers valuable guidance and counsel to Lord Rama and his companions, helping them navigate the complexities of the world and overcome the challenges they face. His wisdom is rooted in his deep understanding of dharma (righteousness) and his unwavering commitment to upholding it in all circumstances.

But Hanuman Ji's wisdom goes beyond mere intellectual knowledge—it is also infused with spiritual insight and divine grace. He draws upon the wisdom of the sages and scriptures, as well as his own inner realization of the truth, to offer profound teachings that resonate deeply with all who hear them.

One of the most notable instances of Hanuman Ji's wisdom is his role in locating Sita, Lord Rama's beloved wife, who has been abducted by the demon king Ravana. Through his intelligence, resourcefulness, and spiritual insight, he is able to locate Sita and deliver Lord Rama's message of hope and reassurance to her, restoring her faith and confidence in the divine plan.

Throughout his interactions with Lord Rama and his companions, Hanuman Ji offers valuable teachings on various aspects of dharma, righteousness, and spirituality. He emphasizes the importance of humility, selflessness, and devotion in the pursuit of spiritual growth, inspiring devotees to cultivate these qualities in their own lives.

But perhaps the greatest lesson that Hanuman Ji imparts is the importance of surrendering oneself completely to the will of the divine. He teaches that true wisdom lies not in intellectual knowledge alone, but in the ability to surrender one's ego and desires to the divine will, trusting in the higher wisdom and guidance of the universe.

As we reflect on Hanuman Ji's role as the messenger of wisdom, let us remember the timeless lessons that he imparts to us—that true knowledge is rooted in spiritual insight and divine grace, and that true wisdom lies in surrendering oneself completely to the will of the divine. For in the heart of every devotee beats the spirit of Hanuman Ji—a spirit that guides us ever onward on the path of righteousness and enlightenment.

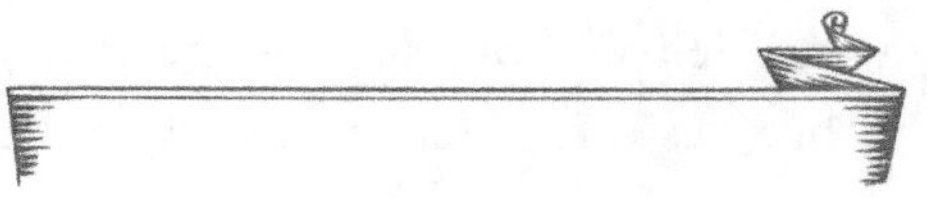

The Eternal Presence: Everlasting Influence

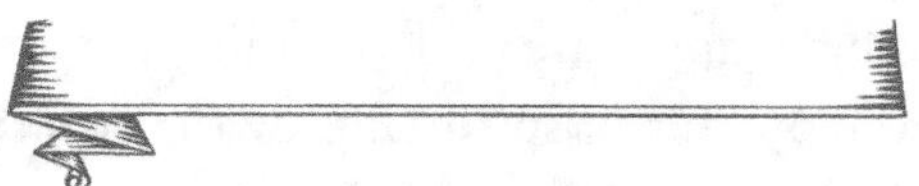

Hanuman Ji's significance extends far beyond the pages of the Ramayana, as his timeless teachings and divine presence continue to inspire and uplift humanity to this day. His eternal influence can be felt in every aspect of life, guiding devotees on the path of righteousness and devotion, and serving as a source of strength and inspiration in times of need.

As the embodiment of devotion, Hanuman Ji's presence is felt in every temple, shrine, and household where his name is revered and his stories are told. Devotees invoke his blessings and seek his guidance in their daily lives, knowing that he is ever-present, watching over them with love and compassion.

But Hanuman Ji's influence goes beyond mere belief or superstition—it is rooted in the profound spiritual truths that he embodies. His teachings on devotion, courage, humility, and service resonate deeply with all who hear them, inspiring them to live a life of righteousness and virtue.

Through his example, Hanuman Ji teaches us the importance of unwavering faith and devotion in the face of adversity, reminding us that no obstacle is too great to overcome with the grace of the divine. He shows us that true greatness lies not in power or prestige, but in the depth of our love and devotion to the divine.

In times of darkness and despair, Hanuman Ji serves as a beacon of light, guiding us out of the depths of ignorance and illusion and leading us towards the path of truth and enlightenment. His divine presence fills us with hope and courage, reminding us that we are never alone in our struggles.

As we reflect on the everlasting influence of Hanuman Ji, let us remember the timeless lessons that he imparts to us—that true greatness lies not in the recognition we receive or the power we wield, but in the depth of our love and devotion to the divine. For in the heart of every devotee beats the spirit of Hanuman Ji—a spirit that inspires us to live a life of righteousness, courage, and devotion in all that we do.

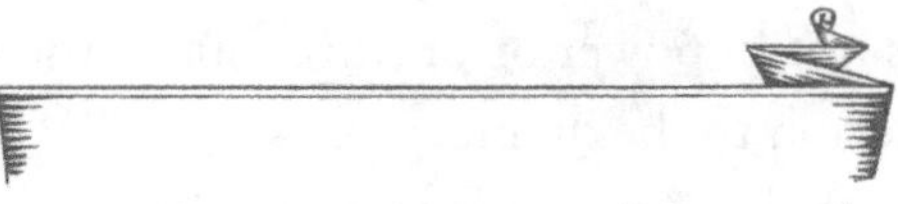

Poem:

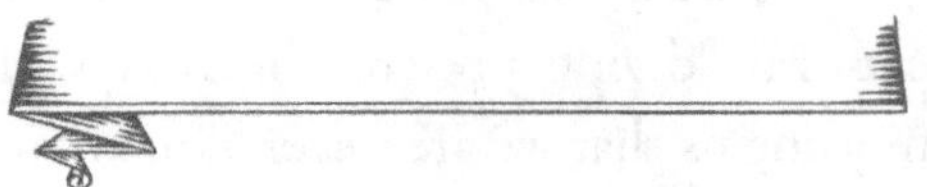

In lands afar, where legends roam,
There dwells a spirit, pure as foam.
With heart aglow and strength untold,
Hanuman Ji, of tales of old.
A warrior bold, with courage rare,
In every heart, he plants a prayer.
With every leap, across the sky,
He echoes truth, to glorify.
In darkest hour, when shadows creep,
His light shines bright, a promise to keep.
With every deed, in every test,
He stands as guardian, ever blessed.
With wisdom deep, beyond compare,
He guides us through, with tender care.
In every trial, in every plight,
He leads us towards eternal light.
Oh Hanuman Ji, with love so true,
We sing your praise, in skies of blue.
For in your heart, our spirits soar,
Forevermore, for evermore.
Jai Hanuman! Jai Shri Ram!

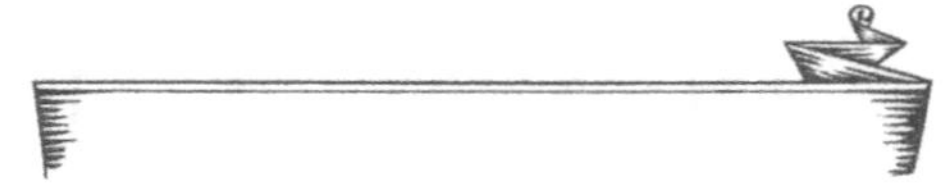

Hanuman Ji's Temples and Worship

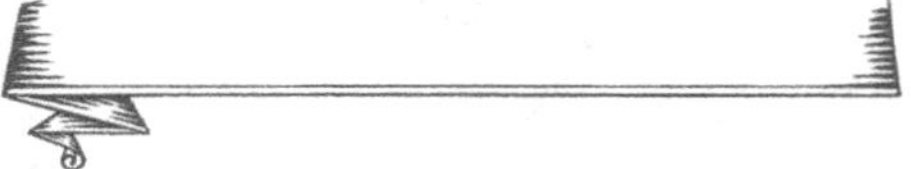

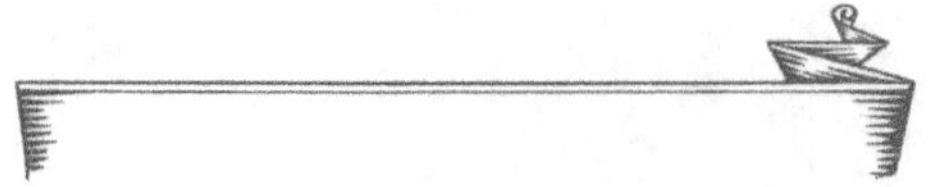

The Sacred Abodes: Origins and Significance

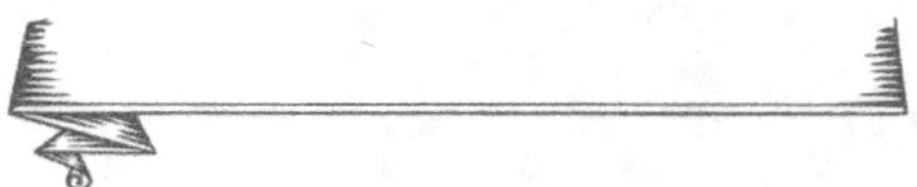

Hanuman Ji's temples stand as sacred abodes where devotees gather to pay homage to the beloved deity, seeking his blessings and divine grace. These temples hold a special significance in Hindu culture, serving as places of worship, pilgrimage, and spiritual solace for millions of devotees worldwide.

The origins of Hanuman Ji's temples can be traced back to ancient times, with the earliest mentions found in Hindu scriptures and epics. As the devotee of Lord Rama and a revered figure in Hindu mythology, Hanuman Ji's popularity grew over the centuries, leading to the establishment of numerous temples dedicated to his worship across India and beyond.

The significance of Hanuman Ji's temples lies in their role as centers of devotion and spiritual upliftment. Devotees flock to these sacred sites to offer prayers, perform rituals, and seek blessings from the divine presence of Hanuman Ji. The atmosphere is charged with bhakti (devotion) and reverence, as devotees express their love and gratitude towards their beloved deity.

Each Hanuman Ji temple is unique in its architecture, rituals, and traditions, reflecting the cultural diversity and spiritual heritage of the region in which it is located. Some temples are grand and majestic, adorned with intricate carvings and sculptures depicting scenes from the Ramayana, while others are simple and humble, serving as quiet retreats for prayer and meditation.

But regardless of their size or grandeur, all Hanuman Ji temples share a common purpose—to provide a sacred space where devotees can connect with the divine presence of Hanuman Ji and experience his love, protection, and guidance in their lives.

In addition to serving as places of worship, Hanuman Ji's temples also play a significant role in community life, serving as centers for social and cultural activities. Festivals and celebrations are held throughout the year to honor Hanuman Ji, drawing devotees from far and wide to participate in the joyous festivities and express their devotion to the beloved deity.

But perhaps the most profound aspect of Hanuman Ji's temples is their role as places of spiritual solace and refuge for devotees in times of need. Whether facing personal challenges, health issues, or other difficulties, devotees turn to Hanuman Ji for strength, courage, and divine intervention, seeking solace and guidance in their darkest hours.

As we reflect on the origins and significance of Hanuman Ji's temples, let us remember the timeless teachings that they impart to us—that true devotion knows no bounds, and that the divine presence of Hanuman Ji resides in the hearts of all who seek him with sincerity and love. For in the sacred abodes of Hanuman Ji, devotees find solace, inspiration, and divine grace to guide them on their spiritual journey.

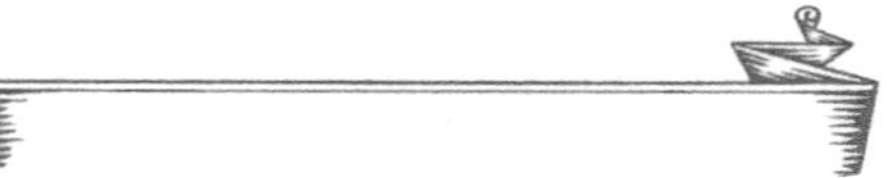

Architecture and Iconography: Divine Manifestations in Stone

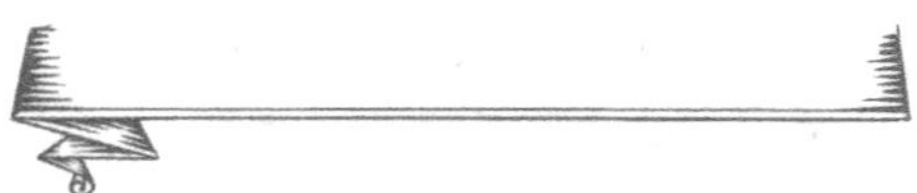

Hanuman Ji's temples are not merely places of worship, but also architectural marvels that showcase intricate craftsmanship and divine iconography. From ancient shrines to modern-day marvels, these temples are adorned with exquisite sculptures, paintings, and carvings that depict the divine presence of Hanuman Ji in all his glory.

The architecture of Hanuman Ji's temples varies greatly depending on the region and time period in which they were built. In North India, temples dedicated to Hanuman Ji often feature a distinctive style known as Nagara architecture, characterized by tall spires (shikharas) and intricate carvings depicting scenes from the Ramayana and other Hindu epics.

In South India, Hanuman Ji's temples often follow the Dravidian style of architecture, characterized by massive gopurams (towering gateways) adorned with colorful sculptures and intricate carvings. These temples are often built with stone and feature elaborate mandapas (pillared halls) where devotees gather for worship and prayer.

But regardless of their architectural style, all Hanuman Ji temples are adorned with sacred symbols and iconography that represent the divine attributes of the beloved deity. Hanuman

Ji is often depicted in various forms, including Anjaneya (the son of Anjana), Pavanputra (the son of the wind god), and Mahavira (the great hero).

One of the most iconic representations of Hanuman Ji is as a monkey-faced deity with a muscular physique, holding a mace (gada) in one hand and a mountain (Parvat) in the other. This image symbolizes his immense strength and power, as well as his unwavering devotion to Lord Rama.

In addition to his physical attributes, Hanuman Ji is also depicted with various symbolic elements that convey deeper spiritual meanings. These include his tilak (sacred mark) on his forehead, which is said to contain the name of Lord Rama, as well as his tail, which represents his loyalty and servitude to his beloved lord.

Inside Hanuman Ji's temples, devotees often find sanctum sanctorums (garbhagrihas) where the main deity is enshrined, along with smaller shrines dedicated to other deities and divine beings. These sanctuaries serve as focal points for worship and meditation, allowing devotees to connect with the divine presence of Hanuman Ji in a sacred and serene environment.

As we marvel at the architectural beauty and divine iconography of Hanuman Ji's temples, let us remember the timeless truths that they symbolize—that the divine presence of Hanuman Ji resides not only in stone and mortar, but also in the hearts of all who seek him with love and devotion. For in the sacred spaces of Hanuman Ji's temples, devotees find inspiration, solace, and divine grace to guide them on their spiritual journey.

Pilgrimage and Sacred Sites: Journeying to Divine Presence

Hanuman Ji's temples serve as sacred destinations for millions of devotees who embark on pilgrimages to seek his blessings and divine grace. These pilgrimage sites are not only places of worship, but also spiritual landmarks that hold deep significance in the hearts and minds of devotees, inspiring them to embark on journeys of devotion and self-discovery.

Throughout India and beyond, there are numerous Hanuman Ji temples that are revered as pilgrimage sites, each with its own unique history, traditions, and spiritual significance. From ancient shrines nestled in remote forests to grand temples located in bustling cities, these sacred sites draw devotees from all walks of life who seek to connect with the divine presence of Hanuman Ji.

One of the most revered pilgrimage sites dedicated to Hanuman Ji is the Hanuman Dhara Temple in Chitrakoot, Uttar Pradesh. Perched atop a hill overlooking the sacred town of Chitrakoot, this temple is believed to be the spot where Hanuman Ji rested while carrying the Sanjeevani herb to save Lord Lakshmana's life during the battle with Ravana. Devotees climb the steep steps leading to the temple to offer prayers and seek blessings from the divine presence of Hanuman Ji.

Another renowned pilgrimage site is the Hanuman Garhi Temple in Ayodhya, Uttar Pradesh, which is believed to be the birthplace of Hanuman Ji. Situated atop a hill overlooking the city, this temple is dedicated to Hanuman Ji in his infant form, and devotees flock here to seek his blessings for courage, strength, and protection.

In addition to these major pilgrimage sites, there are countless other Hanuman Ji temples scattered across India and beyond, each with its own unique significance and spiritual allure. Devotees undertake arduous journeys to visit these sacred sites, often walking long distances and enduring physical hardships in their quest for divine grace.

But regardless of the distance traveled or the challenges faced, the pilgrimage to a Hanuman Ji temple is more than just a physical journey—it is a spiritual odyssey that deepens one's connection with the divine and strengthens one's faith and devotion. It is a journey of self-discovery and transformation, where devotees surrender themselves completely to the divine will and experience the infinite love and grace of Hanuman Ji.

As we embark on our own spiritual pilgrimage to the sacred sites of Hanuman Ji, let us remember the timeless teachings that they impart to us—that true devotion knows no bounds, and that the divine presence of Hanuman Ji resides not only in temples and shrines, but also in the hearts of all who seek him with sincerity and love. For in the journey to Hanuman Ji's sacred abodes, devotees find inspiration, solace, and divine grace to guide them on their spiritual path.

Festivals and Celebrations: Joyous Commemorations of Devotion

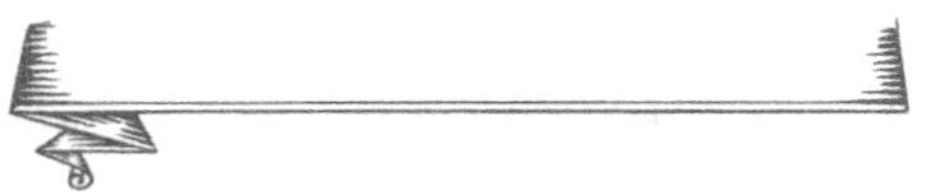

Hanuman Ji's temples are not only places of worship but also vibrant centers of celebration and festivity, where devotees come together to honor the beloved deity through joyous rituals, ceremonies, and cultural events. Throughout the year, these temples come alive with the sounds of bhajans (devotional songs), the aroma of incense, and the fervent prayers of devotees, as they commemorate the divine presence of Hanuman Ji in their lives.

One of the most joyous celebrations dedicated to Hanuman Ji is Hanuman Jayanti, which marks the birth anniversary of the beloved deity. This auspicious occasion is celebrated with great fervor and devotion in Hanuman Ji's temples across India and beyond, with devotees gathering to offer prayers, chant hymns, and participate in processions and rituals that commemorate the divine birth of Hanuman Ji.

During Hanuman Jayanti, devotees adorn Hanuman Ji's temples with flowers, garlands, and colorful decorations, creating a festive atmosphere that fills the air with joy and devotion. Special ceremonies and rituals are performed throughout the day, including the recitation of Hanuman Chalisa (a hymn dedicated to Hanuman Ji), the offering of prasad (sacred food), and the reading of scriptures that narrate the divine exploits of Hanuman Ji.

Another important festival dedicated to Hanuman Ji is Hanuman Vrat, which is observed by devotees with fasting, prayers, and acts of devotion to seek the blessings and protection of Hanuman Ji. This vrat is often observed on Tuesdays, which is considered auspicious for worshiping Hanuman Ji, and devotees abstain from consuming grains and other foods as a form of penance and purification.

In addition to these major festivals, Hanuman Ji's temples also celebrate various other auspicious occasions throughout the year, including Ram Navami (the birthday of Lord Rama), Diwali (the festival of lights), and Navratri (the nine nights dedicated to the divine mother). These celebrations bring devotees together in a spirit of unity and devotion, fostering a sense of community and camaraderie among all who gather to honor the divine presence of Hanuman Ji.

But perhaps the most profound aspect of these festivals and celebrations is their ability to unite devotees from all walks of life in a shared expression of devotion and gratitude towards Hanuman Ji. Regardless of caste, creed, or social status, devotees come together as one family to celebrate the divine presence of Hanuman Ji and seek his blessings for peace, prosperity, and spiritual upliftment.

As we immerse ourselves in the joyous celebrations of Hanuman Ji's festivals, let us remember the timeless teachings that they impart to us—that true devotion transcends barriers of caste, creed, and social status, and that the divine presence of Hanuman Ji resides in the hearts of all who seek him with sincerity and love. For in the joyous festivities of Hanuman Ji's temples, devotees find inspiration, solace, and divine grace to guide them on their spiritual journey.

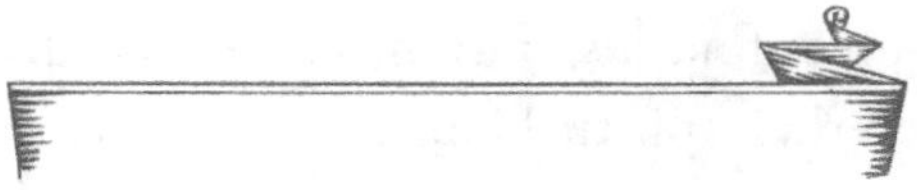

Service and Philanthropy: Compassion in Action

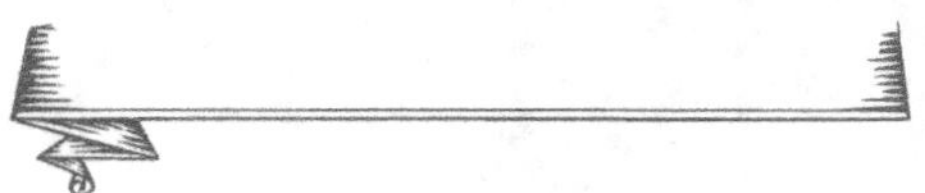

Hanuman Ji's temples serve not only as places of worship and celebration but also as centers of compassion and philanthropy, where devotees come together to serve those in need and uplift the less fortunate in society. Inspired by the selfless example of Hanuman Ji, devotees engage in various acts of seva (service) and charity, embodying the spirit of compassion and kindness that lies at the heart of his teachings.

One of the most common forms of service offered in Hanuman Ji's temples is the distribution of prasad (sacred food) to devotees and visitors. Volunteers prepare and distribute nutritious meals, snacks, and sweets to all who come to the temple, regardless of their background or circumstances. This act of seva not only nourishes the body but also nourishes the soul, fostering a sense of unity and goodwill among all who partake in it.

In addition to providing food, Hanuman Ji's temples also offer various other forms of assistance to those in need, including medical care, education, and financial support. Free medical camps and clinics are often organized in temple premises, where devotees can receive healthcare services and medicines free of charge. Scholarships and educational programs are also offered to underprivileged children, empowering them to pursue their dreams and build a brighter future for themselves and their families.

Hanuman Ji's temples also play a vital role in disaster relief and humanitarian aid efforts, providing assistance to communities affected by natural disasters, such as floods, earthquakes, and cyclones. Volunteers mobilize resources and coordinate relief efforts to provide food, shelter, and medical care to those in need, embodying the spirit of seva and selflessness that Hanuman Ji exemplifies.

But perhaps the most profound aspect of service in Hanuman Ji's temples is its transformative impact on both the giver and the receiver. By engaging in acts of seva and philanthropy, devotees cultivate virtues such as compassion, empathy, and selflessness, while also deepening their connection with the divine presence of Hanuman Ji. And for those who receive assistance, the kindness and generosity of others serve as a ray of hope in their darkest hour, reminding them that they are not alone in their struggles.

As we reflect on the spirit of service and philanthropy in Hanuman Ji's temples, let us remember the timeless teachings that they impart to us—that true greatness lies not in wealth or power, but in the ability to serve others with love and compassion. For in the compassionate actions of Hanuman Ji's devotees, we see the divine presence of Hanuman Ji shining brightly, illuminating the path of service and selflessness for all who seek to follow it.

Global Reach and Influence: Spreading Devotion Across Boundaries

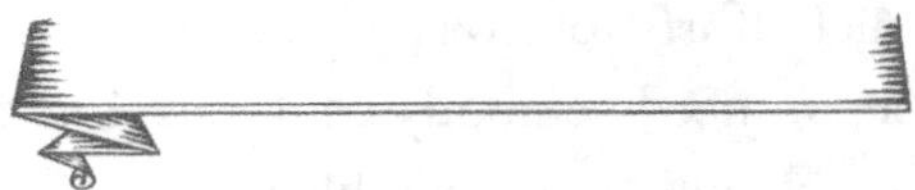

Hanuman Ji's temples are not confined to a single region or country but have a global presence, with devotees from diverse backgrounds and cultures coming together to worship and honor the beloved deity. From India to the farthest corners of the world, Hanuman Ji's temples serve as beacons of light, spreading devotion and inspiring millions of people to embrace the teachings and values of Hanuman Ji.

In recent years, there has been a growing interest in Hanuman Ji's worship outside of India, with temples dedicated to the beloved deity springing up in countries such as the United States, Canada, the United Kingdom, Australia, and many others. These temples serve as spiritual hubs for the Indian diaspora and other devotees who seek to connect with the divine presence of Hanuman Ji in their adopted homelands.

The global reach of Hanuman Ji's temples is a testament to the enduring appeal and universal significance of his teachings, which transcend cultural, linguistic, and geographical boundaries. Devotees from all walks of life are drawn to the timeless message of devotion, courage, and selflessness embodied by Hanuman Ji, finding solace and inspiration in his divine presence wherever they may be.

In addition to physical temples, Hanuman Ji's worship has also found expression in the digital realm, with online platforms and social media channels dedicated to spreading devotion and knowledge about the beloved deity. Devotees from around the world connect virtually to share prayers, stories, and experiences, fostering a sense of community and camaraderie that transcends physical distance.

But perhaps the most profound aspect of Hanuman Ji's global reach is its ability to foster unity and harmony among people of different cultures and faiths. Regardless of their background or beliefs, devotees from diverse backgrounds come together in Hanuman Ji's temples to worship and seek his blessings, embracing a spirit of mutual respect, understanding, and acceptance.

As we celebrate the global reach and influence of Hanuman Ji's temples, let us remember the timeless teachings that they impart to us—that true devotion knows no boundaries, and that the divine presence of Hanuman Ji resides in the hearts of all who seek him with sincerity and love. For in the global network of Hanuman Ji's temples, devotees find inspiration, solace, and divine grace to guide them on their spiritual journey.

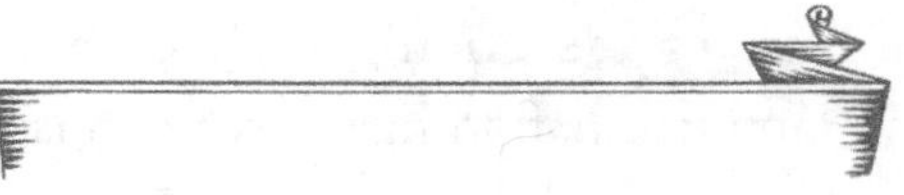

Poem:

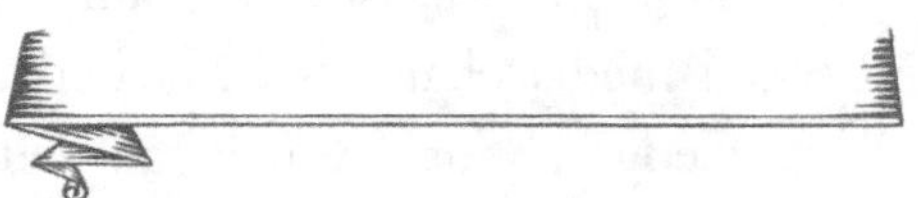

In lands afar, where cultures blend,
Hanuman's love, it knows no end.
From distant shores, to mountain peaks,
His name resounds, where devotion speaks.
In temples grand, with spires high,
Devotees raise their voices nigh.
With hymns of praise, and hearts aglow,
They worship Hanuman, whom they know.
In every heart, his presence felt,
A beacon bright, where shadows melt.
With boundless love, and courage bold,
He guides us on, through paths untold.
In times of need, we call his name,
And feel his grace, a sacred flame.
With every leap, across the sky,
He hears our prayers, our spirits high.
Oh Hanuman Ji, with love divine,
In every heart, your light shall shine.
In temples vast, and lands afar,
Your presence fills us, like a star.
So let us sing, with voices strong,
The glory of Hanuman's song.

For in his love, we find our way,
Forevermore, from day to day.
Jai Hanuman! Jai Shri Ram!
In every heart, your love we clam.

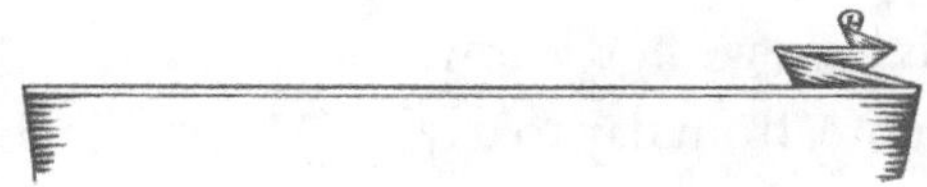

Hanuman Ji's Teachings and Values

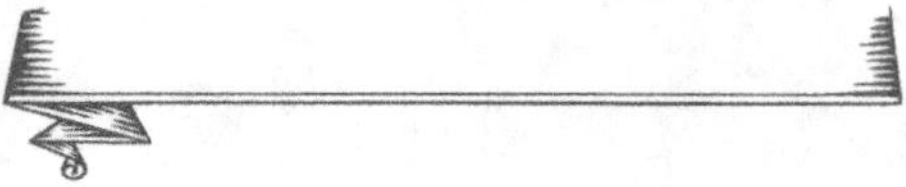

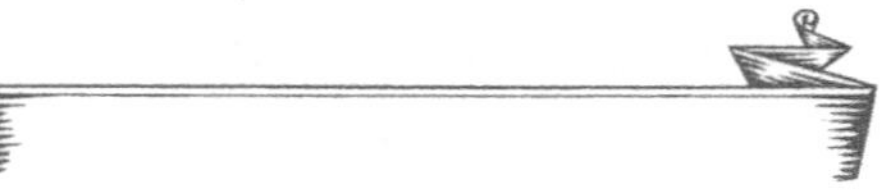

Pathways to Enlightenment: Devotion and Surrender

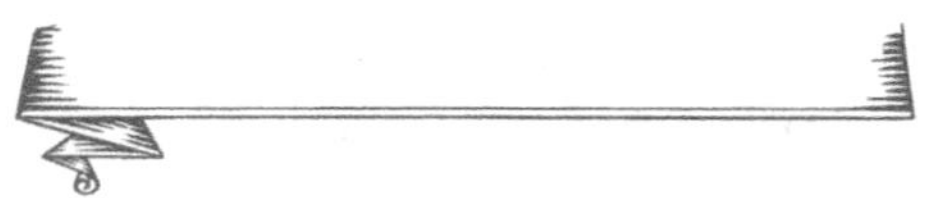

Hanuman Ji's teachings are a timeless guidebook for spiritual seekers, offering profound insights and practical wisdom to navigate the journey of life with grace and purpose. At the heart of Hanuman Ji's teachings lie the virtues of devotion and surrender, which form the cornerstone of his spiritual philosophy and serve as pathways to enlightenment.

Devotion, or bhakti, is the central theme of Hanuman Ji's teachings, emphasizing the importance of cultivating a deep and unwavering love for the divine. Hanuman Ji himself exemplifies the highest form of devotion, as he wholeheartedly dedicates himself to the service of Lord Rama, his beloved master, with boundless love and loyalty.

Through his devotion to Lord Rama, Hanuman Ji teaches us that true fulfillment and inner peace can only be found in the selfless service of the divine. He inspires us to transcend our ego and desires, and to surrender ourselves completely to the will of the divine, trusting in the higher wisdom and guidance of the universe.

But surrender, or samarpan, does not imply passivity or resignation. Instead, it is an active process of letting go of our attachment to outcomes and relinquishing control to the divine will. Hanuman Ji teaches us that true surrender is not a sign of weakness, but rather a source of strength and empowerment, as it allows us to align our actions with the greater purpose of the universe.

Through the practice of devotion and surrender, Hanuman Ji shows us how to live a life of purpose and meaning, rooted in the timeless values of love, humility, and service. He teaches us that true greatness lies not in power or prestige, but in the depth of our love and devotion to the divine, and in our willingness to serve others with compassion and kindness.

In the words of Hanuman Ji himself, "He who surrenders himself to the divine will, finds peace and contentment in all circumstances." These words encapsulate the essence of Hanuman Ji's teachings, reminding us that true fulfillment and happiness can only be found in surrendering ourselves completely to the divine presence within and around us.

As we reflect on the teachings of Hanuman Ji, let us remember the timeless wisdom that he imparts to us—that true fulfillment and inner peace can only be found in the practice of devotion and surrender to the divine will. For in the footsteps of Hanuman Ji, we find the pathway to enlightenment and liberation from the bonds of suffering and ignorance.

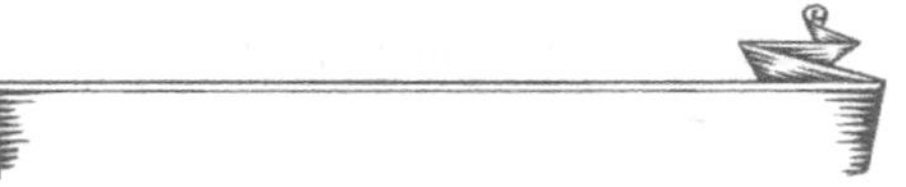

Courage and Strength: Embracing Fearlessness and Resilience

Hanuman Ji's teachings on courage and strength serve as a beacon of inspiration for all who face challenges and obstacles on their spiritual journey. Through his fearless exploits and unwavering determination, Hanuman Ji demonstrates the transformative power of courage and resilience in overcoming adversity and achieving greatness.

Courage, or veerata, is a central theme in Hanuman Ji's teachings, embodying the fearless spirit that enables one to confront and conquer the trials and tribulations of life. Hanuman Ji's courage knows no bounds, as he fearlessly confronts powerful adversaries, leaps across oceans, and even carries mountains in service to his beloved master, Lord Rama.

Through his fearless actions, Hanuman Ji teaches us that true courage is not the absence of fear, but rather the ability to act in spite of it. He inspires us to face our fears head-on, to embrace challenges with confidence and determination, and to trust in our inner strength and resilience to see us through even the darkest of times.

Strength, or bal, is another key aspect of Hanuman Ji's teachings, symbolizing the physical, mental, and spiritual fortitude needed to overcome obstacles and achieve one's goals.

Hanuman Ji's strength is legendary, as he possesses the power to uproot trees, crush mountains, and overcome any obstacle that stands in his way.

But Hanuman Ji's strength is not just brute force—it is tempered by wisdom, humility, and compassion. He uses his strength not for personal gain or glory, but in service to others and in devotion to the divine. Through his example, Hanuman Ji teaches us that true strength lies not in the muscles, but in the heart, where love, courage, and compassion reside.

In the words of Hanuman Ji himself, "Strength does not come from physical capacity. It comes from an indomitable will." These words remind us that true strength is not measured by outward appearances or material possessions, but by the depth of our resolve and the clarity of our purpose.

As we reflect on the teachings of Hanuman Ji on courage and strength, let us remember the timeless wisdom that he imparts to us—that true greatness lies not in the absence of fear or adversity, but in the courage and resilience to overcome them. For in the footsteps of Hanuman Ji, we find the strength to face life's challenges with grace and determination, knowing that we are supported by the divine presence within and around us.

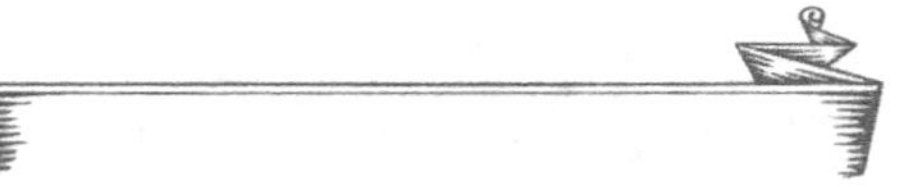

Humility and Service: Embracing Humility and Selfless Service

Hanuman Ji's teachings on humility and service are a testament to the transformative power of selflessness and compassion in fostering spiritual growth and inner fulfillment. Through his humble demeanor and tireless dedication to the service of others, Hanuman Ji exemplifies the highest ideals of humility and selfless service, inspiring all who seek to follow in his footsteps.

Humility, or vinay, is a fundamental aspect of Hanuman Ji's character, as he embodies the virtues of modesty, humility, and self-effacement in all his actions. Despite his immense strength and power, Hanuman Ji remains humble and unassuming, never seeking recognition or praise for his heroic deeds, but rather performing them out of pure love and devotion to his beloved master, Lord Rama.

Through his example, Hanuman Ji teaches us that true greatness lies not in pride or arrogance, but in humility and selflessness. He shows us that humility is not a sign of weakness, but rather a source of strength and grace, allowing us to connect more deeply with others and with the divine presence within and around us.

Service, or seva, is another key aspect of Hanuman Ji's teachings, emphasizing the importance of selfless action in serving others and alleviating their suffering. Hanuman Ji's life is a testament to the transformative power of service, as he tirelessly serves Lord Rama and his companions with unwavering dedication and devotion, putting their needs above his own at every turn.

Through his example, Hanuman Ji teaches us that true fulfillment and inner peace can only be found in selfless service to others. He inspires us to transcend our own selfish desires and ego-driven ambitions, and to dedicate ourselves wholeheartedly to the welfare and happiness of others, regardless of their background or circumstances.

In the words of Hanuman Ji himself, "He who serves others with humility and devotion, finds true happiness and fulfillment in life." These words remind us that true happiness and fulfillment can only be found in selfless service to others, and in the humility to recognize the divine presence in all beings.

As we reflect on the teachings of Hanuman Ji on humility and service, let us remember the timeless wisdom that he imparts to us—that true greatness lies not in power or prestige, but in the depth of our humility and the sincerity of our service to others. For in the footsteps of Hanuman Ji, we find the pathway to spiritual growth, inner fulfillment, and divine grace.

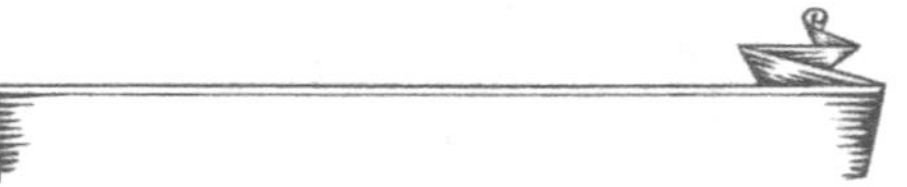

Devotion to Duty: Fulfilling Responsibilities with Dedication

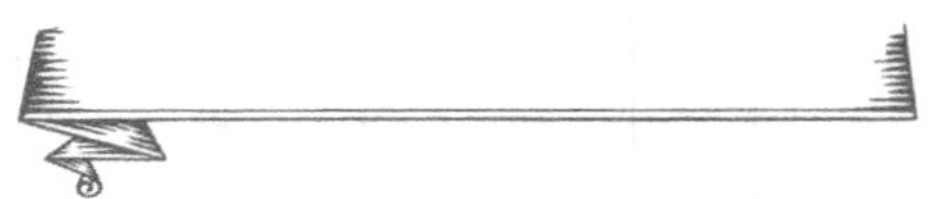

Hanuman Ji's teachings on devotion to duty serve as a guiding light for all who seek to fulfill their responsibilities with dedication and integrity. Through his unwavering commitment to serving his beloved master, Lord Rama, Hanuman Ji exemplifies the highest ideals of duty and loyalty, inspiring all who encounter his story to embrace their own responsibilities with diligence and devotion.

Duty, or dharma, is a central theme in Hanuman Ji's teachings, emphasizing the importance of fulfilling one's responsibilities and obligations in life. Hanuman Ji's entire life is a testament to his unwavering commitment to his duty as a servant and devotee of Lord Rama, as he selflessly dedicates himself to serving his master with love, loyalty, and devotion.

Through his example, Hanuman Ji teaches us that true fulfillment and inner peace can only be found in embracing our responsibilities with dedication and sincerity. He inspires us to rise above our own selfish desires and ego-driven ambitions, and to prioritize the welfare and happiness of others above our own comfort and convenience.

Loyalty, or samarpan, is another key aspect of Hanuman Ji's teachings, emphasizing the importance of remaining steadfast and true to one's commitments and relationships. Hanuman Ji's unwavering loyalty to Lord Rama is legendary, as he remains by his side through thick and thin, facing countless challenges and adversities with courage and determination.

Through his example, Hanuman Ji teaches us that true loyalty is not just a matter of words or promises, but of actions and deeds. He shows us that loyalty is not blind obedience, but a conscious choice to stand by those we love and respect, even in the face of hardship or adversity.

In the words of Hanuman Ji himself, "He who fulfills his duties with dedication and devotion, finds true fulfillment and happiness in life." These words remind us that true fulfillment and happiness can only be found in embracing our responsibilities with dedication and sincerity, and in serving others with love and loyalty.

As we reflect on the teachings of Hanuman Ji on devotion to duty, let us remember the timeless wisdom that he imparts to us—that true greatness lies not in the pursuit of personal gain or glory, but in the selfless service of others and the unwavering commitment to one's duty. For in the footsteps of Hanuman Ji, we find the pathway to spiritual growth, inner fulfillment, and divine grace.

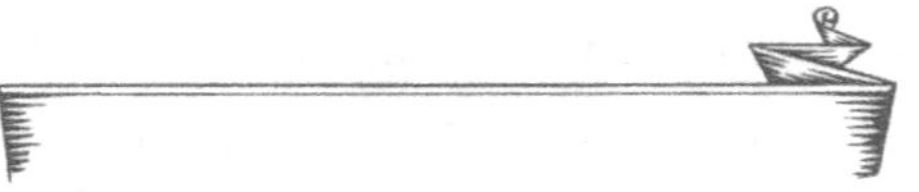

Integrity and Truthfulness: Upholding Moral Values and Ethical Principles

Hanuman Ji's teachings on integrity and truthfulness serve as a moral compass for all who strive to uphold ethical principles and live a life of integrity. Through his unwavering commitment to truth and righteousness, Hanuman Ji exemplifies the highest ideals of integrity and honesty, inspiring all who encounter his story to embrace these virtues in their own lives.

Integrity, or satya, is a central theme in Hanuman Ji's teachings, emphasizing the importance of upholding moral values and ethical principles in all aspects of life. Hanuman Ji's integrity is unshakable, as he remains steadfast in his commitment to truth and righteousness, even in the face of temptation and adversity.

Through his example, Hanuman Ji teaches us that true fulfillment and inner peace can only be found in living a life of integrity and honesty. He inspires us to stand firm in our convictions, to speak the truth with courage and conviction, and to uphold moral values and ethical principles in all our thoughts, words, and actions.

Truthfulness, or satyavachan, is another key aspect of Hanuman Ji's teachings, emphasizing the importance of speaking the truth and honoring one's word. Hanuman Ji's words are imbued with the power of truth, as he speaks only what is necessary and true, and never deviates from the path of righteousness.

Through his example, Hanuman Ji teaches us that true strength lies not in deception or manipulation, but in the power of truth and honesty. He shows us that truthfulness is not just a matter of words, but of integrity and authenticity in all our interactions and relationships.

In the words of Hanuman Ji himself, "He who upholds truth and integrity in all his actions, finds true fulfillment and happiness in life." These words remind us that true fulfillment and happiness can only be found in living a life of integrity and honesty, and in upholding moral values and ethical principles in all our thoughts, words, and deeds.

As we reflect on the teachings of Hanuman Ji on integrity and truthfulness, let us remember the timeless wisdom that he imparts to us—that true greatness lies not in the pursuit of personal gain or glory, but in the unwavering commitment to truth and righteousness. For in the footsteps of Hanuman Ji, we find the pathway to spiritual growth, inner fulfillment, and divine grace.

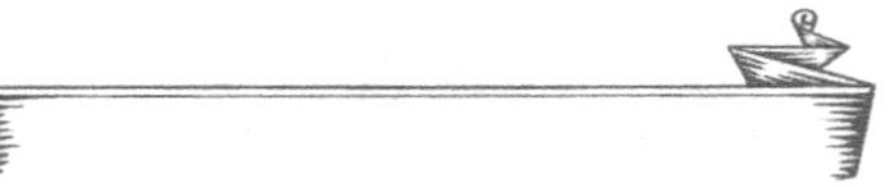

Compassion and Forgiveness: Embracing Compassion and Letting Go of Resentment

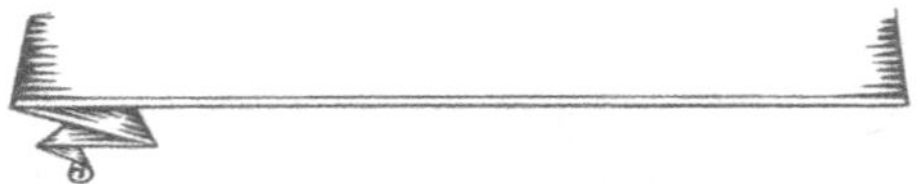

Hanuman Ji's teachings on compassion and forgiveness serve as a guiding light for all who seek to cultivate a heart full of love and empathy towards others. Through his boundless compassion and willingness to forgive, Hanuman Ji exemplifies the highest ideals of kindness and forgiveness, inspiring all who encounter his story to embrace these virtues in their own lives.

Compassion, or karuna, is a central theme in Hanuman Ji's teachings, emphasizing the importance of cultivating empathy and understanding towards all living beings. Hanuman Ji's heart overflows with compassion, as he selflessly serves others and alleviates their suffering with love and kindness, regardless of their background or circumstances.

Through his example, Hanuman Ji teaches us that true fulfillment and inner peace can only be found in cultivating a heart full of compassion and empathy towards others. He inspires us to see the divine presence in all beings, and to treat them with kindness, respect, and understanding, knowing that we are all interconnected in the web of life.

Forgiveness, or kshama, is another key aspect of Hanuman Ji's teachings, emphasizing the importance of letting go of resentment and anger towards others. Hanuman Ji's heart is free from grudges and resentment, as he forgives even his enemies and extends love and compassion to all, regardless of their past actions.

Through his example, Hanuman Ji teaches us that true strength lies not in holding onto anger or resentment, but in the power of forgiveness and compassion. He shows us that forgiveness is not a sign of weakness, but of inner strength and maturity, allowing us to release the burden of resentment and find peace in our hearts.

In the words of Hanuman Ji himself, "He who embraces compassion and forgiveness in all his actions, finds true fulfillment and happiness in life." These words remind us that true fulfillment and happiness can only be found in cultivating a heart full of love and empathy towards others, and in letting go of resentment and anger through the power of forgiveness.

As we reflect on the teachings of Hanuman Ji on compassion and forgiveness, let us remember the timeless wisdom that he imparts to us—that true greatness lies not in the pursuit of personal gain or glory, but in the cultivation of a heart full of love, empathy, and forgiveness towards all beings. For in the footsteps of Hanuman Ji, we find the pathway to spiritual growth, inner fulfillment, and divine grace.

Poem:

In Hanuman's heart, compassion flows,
    A gentle breeze, where kindness grows.
With eyes that see beyond the veil,
He spreads love's light, where shadows pale.
In every heart, his grace resides,
A guiding star, through darkest tides.
With hands that heal and words that soothe,
He offers solace, to those who move.
In Hanuman's heart, forgiveness reigns,
A gentle rain, that washes stains.
With open arms, he welcomes all,
And lifts them up, should they stumble or fall.
In every soul, his love is felt,
A sacred flame, where hope's knelt.
With deeds that speak of mercy's call,
He embraces all, both great and small.
In Hanuman's heart, the world finds peace,
A boundless ocean, where sorrows cease.
With love that knows no bounds or end,
He guides us home, as friend to friend.
So let us walk, in Hanuman's way,
With hearts that sing, and spirits sway.

For in his love, we find our light,
And journey forth, through darkest night.

Conclusion: Embracing the Legacy of Hanuman Ji

In the grand tapestry of Hindu mythology, the figure of Hanuman Ji stands as a towering beacon of devotion, courage, and selflessness. Through his timeless teachings and awe-inspiring deeds, Hanuman Ji has captured the hearts and minds of devotees across generations, inspiring them to embody the highest ideals of love, service, and spiritual awakening.

As we reflect on the myriad facets of Hanuman Ji's legacy, from his unwavering devotion to Lord Rama, to his boundless courage and strength, to his humility, integrity, and compassion, we are reminded of the timeless wisdom and universal truths that he imparts to us.

Hanuman Ji's temples stand as sacred sanctuaries, where devotees gather to seek his blessings and guidance, and to draw inspiration from his divine presence. These temples serve not only as places of worship and devotion but also as centers of compassion and service, where devotees come together to serve those in need and uplift the less fortunate in society.

Hanuman Ji's teachings transcend the boundaries of time, culture, and geography, offering profound insights and practical wisdom to navigate the journey of life with grace and purpose. Whether we seek solace in times of adversity, strength in times of weakness, or guidance in times of doubt, Hanuman Ji's teachings provide us with the light and inspiration we need to overcome obstacles and achieve greatness.

As we embrace the legacy of Hanuman Ji, let us strive to embody the timeless virtues and values that he exemplifies—devotion, courage, humility, integrity, compassion, and forgiveness. Let us walk in his footsteps with humility and reverence, knowing that in his divine presence, we find the pathway to spiritual growth, inner fulfillment, and divine grace.

Jai Hanuman! Jai Shri Ram!

www.ingramcontent.com/pod-product-compliance
Lightning Source LLC
Chambersburg PA
CBHW071320150726
47997CB00002B/537